PACIFIC COAST HIGHWAY IN LOS ANGELES COUNTY

PACIFIC COAST HIGHWAY IN LOS ANGELES COUNTY

Carina Monica Montoya

THE History PRESS

Published by The History Press
Charleston, SC 29403
www.historypress.net

Front cover, top left: Pacific Coast Highway traffic at sunset. *Courtesy of EGD's portfolio, 5707669*; *top right*: Aerial view of Santa Monica Bay. *Copyright Department of Transportation*; *bottom left*: Winding Pacific Coast Highway near Pacific Palisades. *Copyright California Department of Transportation*; *bottom right*: Surfer walking with surfboard by palm trees. *Courtesy of Carol Highsmith Archive/Library of Congress.*
Back cover, top: Santa Monica Pier. *Photo by John Moss*; *bottom*: Surfer riding wave at Redondo Beach. *Photo by John Moss.*

First published 2014

Manufactured in the United States

ISBN 978.1.62619.020.7

Library of Congress CIP data applied for.

Notice: The information in this book is true and complete to the best of our knowledge. It is offered without guarantee on the part of the author or The History Press. The author and The History Press disclaim all liability in connection with the use of this book.

Contents

Foreword, by Robert C. Pavlik 7
Acknowledgements 9
Introduction 11

1. Malibu 15
2. Topanga 27
3. Pacific Palisades and Will Rogers State Beach 35
4. Santa Monica 43
5. Venice Beach and Marina del Rey 57
6. Sepulveda/El Segundo 65
7. South Bay: Manhattan Beach, Hermosa Beach, Redondo Beach and Palos Verdes Peninsula 71
8. Torrance 81
9. Harbor Cities 85
10. Long Beach 91

Conclusion 95
Index 97
About the Author and Photographer 105

Foreword

The Pacific Coast Highway (PCH) is one of the most widely recognized and storied drives in the world. It includes the communities of Long Beach, Santa Monica and Malibu, longtime magnets for millions coming to seek the magical interface between land and water, and reaches from the urban city to the rural region that hugs the rugged western reach of the coastline. It's not always been easy to build and maintain a roadway along this dynamic, ever-changing location. Time, tides, fires, storms, landslides and earthquakes all conspire to sever the tenuous ribbon of asphalt and concrete that links large cities and remote communities and serves many thousands of travelers, residents, tourists and businesses on a daily basis. In Malibu, the friable cliffs are composed of sedimentary rock laid down under an ancient sea and subsequently crushed, folded and uplifted over a period of millions of years. The steep hillsides easily erode, dropping rock and sand (and the occasional large boulder) onto the highway, necessitating a quick cleanup or months of nail-biting, steering wheel–pounding detours while engineers devise strategies to obviate the obstruction. Sometimes a massive retaining wall, complete with steel tendons driven deep into the earth and grouted into place, is the only engineering solution available to maintain a safe and traversable roadway. Soil conditions can vary from location to location, requiring specialized treatment during construction to avoid settlement and cracking of the pavement. The marine environment, which includes salty sea air, sun, rain and fog, can damage and deteriorate steel signs, culverts, structures and guardrails, requiring regular maintenance and periodic replacement to ensure the traveling public's safety. Bridges can take a beating, both from the steady hum of daily traffic as well as the usually placid flow of the streams and rivers they cross, which can swell into raging torrents of water during floods as the rivers rise and the tides swell to scour at the bridges' columns and abutments.

But on a clear day, with a light breeze and warm temperatures, a drive on PCH enjoying the magnificent Malibu coastline is one of life's great pleasures. It's to the credit of several generations of planners, highway engineers, geologists and maintenance personnel that we can access and enjoy this beautiful region on a regular basis.

Robert C. Pavlik
Environmental Planner and Historian
California Department of Transportation
San Luis Obispo, California

Acknowledgements

I want to thank my editors at The History Press, especially Jerry Roberts, for seeing my vision of this book, and special thanks to Julia Turner, project editor, for her professional help, guidance and patience.

I am indebted to Robert C. Pavlik, environmental planner and historian of the California Department of Transportation, for his invaluable knowledge, assistance, generosity and his willingness to write the foreword to this book; Deborah Cismowski, history librarian at Caltrans Transportation Library & History Center, for her professionalism, help and assistance in providing access to hundreds of vintage photographs of Pacific Coast Highway in Los Angeles County; and John Moss, of John Moss Photography, for his talent, skill and professional services.

Special thanks to Lou La Monte, mayor of Malibu, for his written contribution to the book; Matthew W. Roth, Auto Club historian, for generously providing me with information pertaining to the early history of Pacific Coast Highway; and the Library of Congress, for the use of the Jon B. Lovelace Collection of California Photographs collection.

My deepest appreciation goes to Dave Cole, TT POA, for his generous transportation services and "hands-on" involvement in the writing of this book; Lincoln Minor, the "unofficial mayor of Malibu Pier," for his information about Malibu's pier; Will Geer's Theatricum Botanicum for its generous photograph contribution; and John Stebbins and Mikhail Kolesnikov for their fantastic photographs.

Introduction

Comprising around seventy-five miles of mainland coast in Los Angeles County, the northwest coastal area remains largely untouched. Urban development's hand has not yet encroached upon its rugged mountains that reach down to Los Angeles County's rocky, sandy shoreline. Its picturesque coastal shoreline runs uninterrupted from Malibu to Santa Monica.

State Route 1, more commonly called Pacific Coast Highway, runs north–south along most of the coastline. The highway ribbons through some of the most picturesque landscapes and scenic routes, which has led it to become a designated All-American Road.

California has long held the title of innovator and leader in the construction of highway routes. CA-1 was one of its early roads that opened in 1912, spanning over five hundred miles along the Pacific Coast from Mendocino County to San Juan Capistrano.

The history of the construction of the highway is interwoven in the histories of the coastal communities it serves. Built piecemeal in various stages and having several different names through the years, it wasn't until 1964 that the state designated it as Highway 1. In the early years, the coastal road was first called Roosevelt Highway, but it was later designated as Route 60, then changed to Route 3 and again redesignated as Route 101 Alternate. It also has unofficial names, such as Cabrillo Highway and Palisades Beach Road. More confusing is that portions of Pacific Coast Highway disappear, and the highway becomes Interstate 101, then in some areas a street and in other areas a boulevard. But it eventually reverts back to being Pacific Coast Highway.

North of Malibu in the northern portion of Ventura County, Highway 101 becomes the coastal highway. In southern California, Highway 101 was originally called *El Camino Real* (the King's Highway). One of California's early highways, it once comprised several roads that were growing into becoming part of a national transportation network. It, too, is called by different names, such as U.S. Route 101, U.S. Highway 101 or 101 freeway. The U.S. 101 freeway was one of the first highways designated by the Bureau of Public Roads in 1925. It spans from San Diego, California, up to the Canadian border, covering around 1,700 miles. Pacific Coast Highway intersects with two other major highways—the 5 Freeway and U.S. 101. Highway 1 (Pacific Coast Highway) spans around 630 miles of scenic route. Pacific Coast Highway in Los Angeles County passes through the coastal communities of Malibu, Topanga, Pacific Palisades, Santa Monica, Venice Beach, Marina del Rey and the South Bay communities of El Segundo, Manhattan Beach, Redondo Beach, Hermosa Beach, Torrance, the harbor cities and Long Beach.

Pacific Coast Highway was first conceived as being a way to link coastal counties that were difficult to reach so they would become part of the state road network. The first section of the highway was completed in 1913, linking Newport Beach and Laguna Beach, but it took sixteen years to open the highway that linked Santa Barbara to San Diego in 1929. One major delay in opening the highway that would link Topanga to Malibu was caused by the owner of the Malibu land, Frederick Hastings Rindge. Rindge envisioned Malibu as a private "American Riviera," and his wife, May K. Rindge, steadfastly fought to keep railroads and highways out of Malibu, upholding her husband's dream of keeping Malibu private after his death in 1905. Delayed by years of litigation, the portion of highway through Malibu was the last to open. In a heroic attempt to keep Malibu private by not allowing a public road to pass through the land, May Rindge waged a battle against the State of California and the powers of the City of Los Angeles until her efforts eventually failed with the opening of the Roosevelt Highway in 1929, at last linking the communities from Santa Barbara to San Diego.

The famed highway is notorious for landslides, especially as a result of heavy rains. Debris and rocks slide down hillsides and onto the highway, forcing road closures, traffic jams and sometimes destruction of structures and injuries to motorists. It's a perfect example of beauty having a dark side. The beauty of the coastal highway is the landscape that sandwiches it—the shoreline and the mountains. It is the immediate surroundings of rolling hills, cliffs, bluffs and slopes that are prone to land-, mud- and rock slides, including large boulders that have rolled onto the highway.

The coastal terrain between Malibu and Santa Monica largely consists of Miocene and basement rocks that date back millions of years, forming unstable cliffs. But considering that large portions of Pacific Coast Highway were blasted and carved out of solid rock, credit must be given to the California Department of Transportation (Caltrans), the gatekeeper of the highway. Without its ongoing upkeep and maintenance, including areas above the highway, the roads would have deteriorated long ago. Continued improvements to the highway keep it open to serve its many purposes: an access to recreational locations, a path for commuters, a scenic route and an access road for coastal and canyon residents and bicycle enthusiasts. Rubberized asphalt-concrete overlay replaced concrete pavement between Malibu and Santa Monica. The overlay was determined to be a longer-lasting material that would require less maintenance, among many other environmental and safety benefits.

Malibu to Pacific Palisades is rugged and steep because of a continuing uplift of the Santa Monica Mountains and continues to be a troubling area. But because land movement occurs in southern California more than other regions of the country, several factors are to blame in contributing to its instability. Development along cliffs, heavy rainfall and storm runoff are contributing factors that worsen the problem and enable conditions that can trigger a landslide. In coupling these contributory factors with natural erosion along its coastline, construction of a highway under these conditions created a high-maintenance and potentially dangerous stretch of road.

In California, coastal development of both urban and recreational areas into hillsides attracts people to live in these unstable locations. Furthermore, the necessary grading for road construction results in increased slope steepness, and the disturbance of vegetation on hilltops or slopes impedes water absorption, resulting in excessive water runoff. Road signs along the highway that warn of "falling rocks" are there for a reason. Even though small rocks are often seen at the base of a hill or bluff, it is a reminder that large slides typically begin small. A large landslide can generate enough force and momentum to destroy anything in its path, and both landslides and mudflows can occur without warning.

"Mean sea level" is a reference level from which vertical elevation is measured. Coastlines or coastal zones are areas where land meets the sea. One factor that causes change in sea levels is climate change. Climate change can increase storm intensities and wave height, resulting in coastal erosion and storm damage. Seasonal storms and high tides have swept away a significant amount of oceanfront along Broad Beach, one of Malibu's prized beach neighborhoods.

Pacific Coast Highway in California is known worldwide for its beautiful and breathtaking landscapes along the Pacific Coast and is one of Southern California's most heavily traveled highways for recreation and coastal destinations. Although the highway is one of the state's most extravagant maintenance expenditures in keeping a particular road open, all would agree that a drive through Southern California's coast in Los Angeles County is priceless.

Chapter 1
Malibu

When you enter Malibu on the Pacific Coast Highway there is a sign that says, "27 Miles of Scenic Beauty." And that's very true…Malibu is one of the most beautiful places on our coast; mountains lead down to beautiful beaches and seemingly unending vistas. Driving through on the PCH makes you think about the Malibu you've heard about, a place where famous movie and TV stars, musicians, artists, and business people live. And that's true too…Then there is the Malibu we locals call home…Where the car beside you is likely to be a neighbor dropping off their kids for soccer or baseball practice. We are a small town with excellent schools, dedicated teachers and passionate parents. We also have a lively population of senior citizens and longtime residents who came here when it was an inexpensive rural backwater. Malibu is a community of hardworking men and women, doctors, lawyers, teachers, surfers, writers, artists, athletes, students, watermen, plumbers, mechanics and families all trying to preserve our lifestyle and community. We are people who care about our environment. We are responsible stewards of the ocean, beaches and mountains we love and share with 15 million visitors a year. Our Malibu is many things, and we welcome you to enjoy it with us.

—Lou La Monte, Mayor, City of Malibu

Spanning the entire Malibu coast, Pacific Coast Highway is interwoven in the colorful fabric of Malibu's history. The Roosevelt Highway opened in 1929 and created a route from Santa Barbara to San Diego. When the state widened the highway in 1947, it became part of Route 1, more commonly called Pacific Coast Highway. Whether it is winter, spring, summer or fall, a drive on Pacific Coast Highway along the Malibu coast is beautiful.

Pacific Coast Highway at Leo Carrillo State Beach marks the northern Los Angeles County boundary line that winds into Malibu—the pearl of one of California's most prized cities in Los Angeles County. Spanning twenty-one miles of breathtaking scenic coastal highway, its coastline is dotted with magnificent and enchanting beaches that boast a surfing paradise, a romantic getaway and a prime community in which to live. Located northwest of the city of Los Angeles, Malibu is bounded by Ventura County to the north, Topanga Canyon to the south, Santa Monica Mountains to the east and the Pacific Ocean to the west. Blanketed with green rolling hills on which many of its flowers and trees—vibrant colorful mounds of bougainvillea, lavender, yellow poppies, holly, chaparral, coastal sage, coast live oak, flowering ash, California juniper, palm, acacia, pine, sycamore, coastal prickly pear, laurel sumac bushes and a variety of colorful succulents and wild flowers—compose the landscape's palette, Malibu showcases nature's colors and a community that is abundant in beauty and rich in history.

Long before the first European expedition led by Juan Rodríguez Cabrillo in 1542 voyaged up California's coast under the flag of Spain, and before Spanish explorer Gaspar de Portola trekked through the West Coast on an expedition that spanned California's coast from San Diego to Sonoma, native inhabitants of a large area of California's coastal land were Chumash Indians. Malibu was one of several Chumash settlements along California's coast. The Chumash established settlements in the hills and along the coast from San Luis Obispo to Santa Monica, where wild game and seafood were plentiful. Spanish expeditions traveled dirt trails near and along California's coast, which the California State Assembly officially designated in 1959 as the California Mission Trail or Camino Real (the King's Highway) because it linked California's twenty-one missions, presidios and pueblos from Mission San Diego de Alcala in San Diego to Mission San Francisco Solano in Sonoma. However, the expedition could not find a passage through a range that met the sea, which was the Santa Monica Mountains along the Malibu coast. The Chumash named the area Humaliwo, or "where the surf sounds loudly."

With Mexico's independence in 1821, missions became secularized, and mission-owned lands were broken up into large ranchos and granted out for individual landownership or permission for use of the land. The grants or permission to use the land were typically given to former soldiers or their descendants for loyal service during the war. José Bartolemé Tapia, a soldier in the Anza expedition, was given permission to use land that comprised Rancho Topanga Malibu Sequit, which he used for grazing cattle and raising his family. From this era came the Mexican vaqueros who worked on the ranchos. They were the first cowboys who were highly skilled in cattle herding. Early American cowboys learned how to rope and handle cattle from these skilled horsemen, and many of those techniques are still used today.

In 1848, the United States and Mexico signed the Treaty of Guadalupe Hidalgo, which resulted in the end of the Mexican-American War, and Rancho Malibu was sold shortly before California became a state in 1850. The new owner of Rancho Malibu was a Frenchman by the name of Leon Victor Prudhomme, husband of Maria Merced Tapia (the granddaughter of José Bartolemé Tapia). In 1857, an Irishman by the name of Don Matteo Keller accepted a quitclaim deed and paid the Prudhommes the equivalent of nearly ten cents an acre for the entire rancho. Upon Keller's death in 1881, his son, Henry Keller, took possession of the rancho and later sold it to a wealthy Bostonian, Frederick Hastings Rindge, who would become the last owner of the 13,315 acres, which he later expanded to encompass 17,000 acres. His untimely death left his wife, May Rindge, as the new gatekeeper of Malibu. A heroine in her own right, she fought to maintain her husband's wishes to keep Malibu private by creating obstacles that prevented entry onto the land, as well as being involved in years of court litigation that merely delayed the inevitable. Although her physical and financial efforts failed, Frederick Hasting Rindge's vision of Malibu becoming an "American Riviera" succeeded.

Today, Malibu is known for its private and affluent beach community population. It is home to many in the film, television and music industries, among other moguls, and like other affluent areas in Los Angeles County, such as Beverly Hills, Bel Air and Hancock Park to only name a few, the costs associated in living in upscale areas keep it pretty much exclusive. Incorporated in 1991, the city of Malibu's coastline decreased from twenty-seven to twenty-one miles. (This explains the confusion about the actual mileage of Malibu's coastline.) Although California in general is plagued with earthquakes, its coastal communities get a quadruple whammy of earthquakes, fire, intense coastal storms and mudslides. But despite natural disasters that have destroyed some of Malibu's oceanfront and hillside multimillion-dollar homes, the scales seem to tip in favor for those capable of and desiring to live in a Mediterranean-type climate by the ocean in a place called Malibu.

Magnificent Beaches

There are more than a dozen beaches along Pacific Coast Highway in Malibu. Although all state beaches in California are public, many of the smaller beaches located in oceanfront neighborhoods are somewhat private because they can be difficult to access. Most of Malibu's beaches have excellent surf, landscaped with natural tidepools, sand dunes, cliffs, large rocks, caves and spectacular views of the Santa Monica Mountains to the Santa Monica Bay, including Catalina Island on a clear day.

Leo Carrillo Beach (once called Sequit Beach or Secos Beach in the 1930s)—named after Leo Carrillo (1880–1961), an actor who portrayed the character Pancho in the 1950s television series *Cisco Kid*—is located at Mulholland Highway and Pacific Coast Highway. It comprises one and a half miles of beach and has beautiful tidepools and coastal caves and reefs, which make it a water playground for swimmers, surfers, windsurfers and surf-fishing enthusiasts. Robert H. Meyer Memorial Beach, near Encinal Canyon Road, consists of cliff-foot or coves called "pocket beaches" that include the El Pescador, La Piedra and El Matador beaches. The beaches are prized for their secluded areas and cliff-side hiking. El Pescador is ideal for surf fishing and bodyboarding, while La Piedra offers picturesque cliffs, bluffs, reefs and kelp forests and is ideal for snorkeling and scuba diving. El Matador is regarded as one of the most beautiful beaches in Malibu because of its cliffs, sea caves, large rocks, sea stacks (eroded sandstone pillars), kelp forest, summer and winter swells for surfers and its pelican and sea lion residents.

Broad Beach is somewhat shielded by an ultra-exclusive neighborhood, so it can be a little tricky finding a way to it. Pacific Coast Highway once ran directly to Broad Beach, but it has been redirected inland and upslope. The former section of the highway

Shore protection along the coast. Seawalls are shore-based structures used to provide protection and lessen coastal erosion. They are constructed where the sea directly impacts the land along the coast. Their purpose is to protect human habitation from tide and wave action. Constructed from a variety of materials—including reinforced concrete, boulders, steel, vinyl, wood and sandbags—seawalls reflect wave energy back into the sea, which reduces erosion. However, wave reflection from a seawall can lower the sand level of the fronting beach. Also, seawalls may cause erosion of nearby, unprotected coastal areas without seawalls. *Copyright California Department of Transportation.*

has been renamed Broad Beach Road. Comprising over one hundred beachfront homes on 1.1 miles of fine white sand coastline, it is prized for its beautiful sand dunes and tidepools. Despite its beauty, Broad Beach continues to be plagued with disasters, such as a fire in 1978 that severely burned and destroyed many of the oceanfront homes. Seasonal storms and high tides have swept away much of its oceanfront. Sandbags and a rock wall are in place to help weather the elements. Just off Broad Beach is Sea Level Drive. Sea Level Drive is a beautiful and well-known residential area among Malibu locals, and East Sea Level Drive runs along the beach, where colorful gardens line the beach side of the road.

Zuma Beach, off Pacific Coast Highway between Las Virgenes/Malibu Canyon Road and Kanan-Dume Road, is one of Malibu's largest and most popular beaches because of its surf, making it an ideal place for annual surfing and kitesurfing events held at the northern end of the beach. Zuma offers something for everyone who loves the beach: bodysurfing, swimming, windsurfing, fishing, shallow diving and its popular volleyball courts on its wide, flat, white sand beach. It is also a popular filming location for both television and film and has been written about in songs by the Rolling Stones and others.

Point Dume is a promontory, an elevated portion of land extending out into the water, on Malibu's coast. Its long bluff forms the northern end of Santa Monica Bay. The bluff was once covered by native chaparral until the 1940s, when houses began popping up and the land was used to raise cattle and grow lima beans. Today, multimillion-dollar mobile homes and state-of-the-art mansions with spectacular ocean views dot the bluff, and it is considered the largest neighborhood on the Pacific Coast Highway beachfront. Known as the "Malibu Riviera," it is one of the most exclusive and picturesque areas.

Point Dume State Beach is at the northwestern tip of Point Dume. It is prized for its picturesque promontory, cliffs, rocky coves and California gray whale watching during December to mid-April, which is their migration period. Conditions are also good for swimming, surfing, scuba diving and fishing. Rock climbing on top rope is also popular at Point Dume. The Point Dume State Preserve has an ascending trail that leads to a coastal bluff and sand dune. The view from the preserve encompasses all of Santa Monica Bay, which includes the northern Malibu Coast, Santa Monica Mountains and Catalina Island. Below the summit is a boardwalk that has a viewing platform, as well as access to the beach and tidepools. Westward Beach at Point Dume borders Zuma Beach and is located in the heart of Malibu's coastline. It is a popular television and film location because of its landscape. The waves at Westward Beach are strong, so mostly experienced and strong swimmers dive in its challenging waters. Locals and experienced surfers frequent both "Big Dume" where the cliffs meet the shore and "Little Dume," although both are difficult to access because of limited parking and other obstacles. Point Dume is listed as California Historical Landmark No. 965.

Paradise Cove is just south of Point Dume, off Pacific Coast Highway. In the 1930s, whaling boats anchored at the Cove brought in gray, humpback and sperm whales, mostly caught within a mile of Malibu. The Cove has been widely used throughout the years in several commercials, music videos, films and television, such as the popular television show *The Rockford Files*, which ran from 1974 to 1980. Bob Morris's Paradise Cove Beach Café is one of Malibu's longtime popular eateries.

Malibu Lagoon, also known as Surfrider Beach, is off Pacific Coast Highway near the Malibu Pier. It is where Malibu Creek meets the Pacific Ocean, forming a point that makes it a south-facing beach. Its seasonal waves can be high and are perfect for surfing. In the 1960s, it was one of the premier surfing spots along the California coast. Its sandbar lagoon is an estuary for hundreds of species of migrating and native birds, including pelicans, seagulls and mallard and canvasback ducks, among many others.

All of the beaches in Malibu have something unique to offer, such as caves, bluffs, tide pools and privacy. Other private beaches that can be difficult to access include Carbon Beach, known as "Billionaire Beach" because it is also one of the most expensive beach communities on Pacific Coast Highway, and Dan Blocker County Beach, named after the actor who portrayed "Hoss" in the long-running series *Bonanza*, from 1959 to 1973. Other beaches that are more accessible off Pacific Coast Highway include Malibu, Nicholas Canyon, Las Tunas, Lechuza, Escondido, Las Flores, La Costa, Latigo Point, Big Rock, Puerco, Ramirez Canyon (also known as Banning Harbor) and Corral Creek (one of the most photographed beaches). There is no denying that the main attraction of Malibu is its many beaches, and Pacific Coast Highway will lead you to them.

Breathtaking Canyons

Malibu has thirteen canyons. Intersecting Pacific Coast Highway is Decker Canyon Road (Route 23, Military Intelligence Service Memorial Highway, named after the U.S. 100th Infantry Battalion and 442nd Regimental Combat Team, all of whom were Japanese Americans). The highway winds steep and twists through the canyons in the Santa Monica Mountains, where vantage points allow spectacular views of the Pacific Ocean. The canyons are part of the Backbone Trail in the Santa Monica Mountains, crossing ridgelines, chaparral-covered hillsides, dense woods and valleys. The trail is still expanding, with the efforts and vision of public and private agencies, organizations and individuals. Upon its completion, it will comprise sixty-five miles of trails that will connect all the parks, preserves and recreation lands within the Santa Monica National Park, stretching from Point Mugu in Ventura County to Will

Rogers State Historic Park in Santa Monica. Malibu is the Backbone Trail's desired starting point. Its trails attract avid hikers, mountain bikers, equestrians and naturalists.

Malibu Canyon passes through the mountains, and Malibu Canyon Road connects the inland valley to the coast. Spectacular vistas can be seen from vantage points from Latigo Canyon, Bonsall Canyon (part of Zuma Canyon), Trancas Canyon, Zuma Creek, Malibu Creek, Lake Malibu, Solstice Canyon, Lake Enchanto, Ramirez Canyon, Escondido Canyon (Escondido Falls is a must-see) and Carbon Canyon. Encinal Canyon, part of the Backbone Trail, offers challenging trails for hikers and mountain-bike enthusiasts. Zuma Canyon is also part of the Backbone Trail and is one of California's most popular trails for hiking and nature observations. Zuma Canyon comprises the Lower Zuma Canyon, Upper Zuma and Newton Canyon. Hiking in the canyons typically begins near Pacific Coast Highway with an upstream climb over sandstone boulders along Zuma Creek. It was also the site where the vaqueros of Rancho Malibu lived in the early 1900s.

Also from Malibu is the legend of the Wu—a people who inhabited the mountain area before the Chumashes' arrival around 3,000 BC. Unnatural-type formations were found within the Los Angeles County line that edges Ventura. The finds were gulches that resembled sculpted ramparts, stone walls on rocky hills and flat surfaces atop windswept peaks. Chumash legend has it that the Wu were obliterated in a flood. Geologists and oceanographers believe that Malibu's sea level at the end of the last ice age was around two hundred feet lower than its present-day level.

Historical Landmarks and Points of Interest

Malibu Cove Colony is located off Pacific Coast Highway and south of Malibu Road. In the early 1920s, Hollywood celebrities began to lease lots and build vacation homes on the oceanfront land. By the 1930s, the area boomed with many celebrities leasing and building cottages. It became a well-known celebrity community, but at the end of the lease, any improvements to and on the land reverted back to May Rindge, the owner of the Malibu Ranch. After May Rindge sold the oceanfront land, the beach community became known as the

Colony. Today, the Colony is still one of Malibu's most famous areas that showcases multimillion-dollar homes on small lots. The view from the oceanfront homes spans the coastline from Santa Monica to Rancho Palos Verdes and the bluffs of Point Dume.

Malibu Pier, also called Keller's Shelter, is located off Pacific Coast Highway. Constructed in 1905, it facilitated the delivery of railroad ties, equipment and tools for the construction of a railway that would service Malibu Ranch and be utilized to export beef, leather and produce from the ranch. The pier opened to the public in 1934 during an unusual flood of barracuda, which helped fill tables with food during the Great Depression. In the 1970s, the pier offered sportfishing boat rides until its temporary closing in 1994, due to heavy rainstorms. The pier has been the site of many film and television scenes through the years, including a scene from the original 1930s film *King Kong* and the popular television series *Baywatch*, among many others. There is excellent saltwater fishing from the pier, and it is common to see the same familiar faces fishing off the pier almost every day, including Lincoln Minor, dubbed the "unofficial mayor of the Malibu Pier." Lincoln has been fishing off the pier for thirty-five years, and cheerfully provided me with a demonstration of his "secret" pier fishing tactics, saying, "It's all about using the right bait." The pier has been named a County Point of Historical Interest by the California Historical Resources Commission.

Serra Retreat was once the site of May Rindge's unfinished fifty-room mansion atop Laudamus Hill in Malibu Canyon, overlooking the Pacific Ocean. Included in the construction plans in 1928 were three wings to the estate, one for each of her three children and their families. Spending over a half million dollars in materials during the Depression era, together with the exorbitant costs of legal battles she fought to keep Malibu private, May Rindge depleted her finances, and the mansion was never completed. After May Rindge's death in 1941, the Franciscan Order of California purchased the estate and completed the construction. Today, it is still occupied and maintained by the friars and is well known for its religious retreats, conference center and serene ambience.

The Adamson House was built by May Rindge's daughter, Rhoda Rindge Adamson, in 1926 on thirteen acres at Vaquero Point off Pacific Coast Highway. It is most noted for its extensive use of decorative tiles that were manufactured at the family-owned Malibu

Potteries, founded by May Rindge and operated from 1926 to 1932. The potteries were constructed on the beachfront near the pier. During World War II, the U.S. Coast Guard utilized its pool house as Command Post No. 5. There were seven beach patrol stations that spanned from Point Mugu to Big Rock Beach. The Adamson House is now the Malibu Lagoon Museum and is listed as No. 966 on the National Register of Historic Places.

Pepperdine University was originally founded in Los Angeles in 1937 by George Pepperdine, but it was relocated to the Malibu area on Pacific Coast Highway when the Adamson family donated 130 acres to the school in 1968, in the spirit of bringing a higher education institution to Malibu. Pepperdine broke ground in 1971 and reopened its new Malibu location in the fall of 1972. The school later acquired additional land that now encompasses 830 acres, and its campus grounds are landscaped with an ocean of green grass. Its alumni include many noteworthy actors, writers, film and television producers and directors, local and international news anchors, sports figures, musicians, artists, singers, beauty queens, a Miss Universe pageant winner, politicians, judges, justices and lawyers, to name only a few.

Remnants of old Malibu can still be seen along Pacific Coast Highway. The first commercial property in Malibu was built in the 1940s and was located along Pacific Coast Highway at La Costa. Today, vineyards are being cultivated in the Santa Monica Mountains and hills and along Malibu's coast. Vineyards in Malibu date back to 1802 when José Bartolomé Tapia first planted grapevines on the rancho. Eateries along Pacific Coast Highway range from casual to upscale establishments, many of which stand on old Malibu haunts, such as the current location of Geoffrey's Restaurant. Geoffrey's is located where the Holiday House, a hotel built in 1948 by film director Dudley Murphy (1897–1968), offered privacy with ocean views and fireplaces in each room and was a popular choice for celebrities in the early years. Pacific Coast Highway at Las Flores was once the site of the Sea Lion Inn, which was destroyed by fire and reopened in 1996 as Duke's. The highway at Sunset was the site of the Sea Shore Inn, which is now Gladstone's restaurant. The site of the Arch Rock, the result of erosion from waves hitting the rock for thousands of years forming two adjacent sea caves that created an opening, became a passageway between Santa Monica and Malibu and a landmark of the area. It was destroyed in 1906; some say from a violent storm, others suspected that it was blasted away by work crews constructing a railroad. The Arch Rock was located near where the Chart House restaurant sits. The Seacomber along the highway is where McDonald's is today. The highway at Trancas was the location of the Trancas Ropers and Riders, a horse-riding ring that had monthly shows, trail rides and square dancing. Today, the Trancas Ropers and Riders are at the Malibu Equestrian Center. The highway at Trancas was also near the site of oceanfront cottages on Zuma Beach that were demolished to make way for the highway in 1945. The highway at Trancas was also the site of the Malibu Trading Post, a store that offered supplies, refreshments and cocktails. The land where the Trading Post sat was redeveloped in the late 1960s to construct a residential tract where Malibu West sits today. There were once two unique homes built by celebrities (one was in the shape of a boat, the other a lighthouse) that were located on Trancas Beach in the 1930s. Malibu High School sits where fields of tomatoes were once grown. Lachusa Point has been renamed Victoria Point.

Malibu has the best of both worlds—ocean and mountains—far enough from the noise and pollution in the city of Los Angeles yet a close enough drive to it to enjoy all the culture and arts a large city has to offer, and the drive in between the two cities along Pacific Coast Highway can be a scenic vacation in itself.

Chapter 2
Topanga

Although the coastal areas from San Luis Obispo to Santa Monica were predominately inhabited by Chumash settlements, the Tongva tribe, also known as Gabrielino-Tongva, whose territory encompassed the city of Los Angeles and the San Gabriel Mountains area, gave the area its name. Topanga has been interpreted to mean "a place above." Pacific Coast Highway at Old Malibu Road marks the area of Topanga—one of Los Angeles's longtime artistic communities dating back to the 1920s. Situated between state park lands, the south end of Malibu, Pacific Palisades and the Pacific Ocean, its canyons and beach draw people to live there and attract visitors to return. The canyon is also home to wildlife, surrounded by an abundance of California pepper trees, chaparral, oak and colorful families of sunflower, mustard, honeysuckle, geranium, poppy, buttercup, rose and snapdragon, to name only a few. Topanga Canyon can be easily accessed off Pacific Coast Highway at Topanga Canyon Boulevard.

Topanga Creek is the third-largest watershed that enters the Santa Monica Bay at Topanga Beach. Lower Topanga was once a Japanese fishing village in the early 1900s. The Los Angeles Athletic Club, founded in 1880 as the first private club in Los Angeles, once owned over one thousand acres of land comprising the base of Topanga Canyon and Lower Topanga, where it intersects with Pacific Coast Highway and the ocean. The club's philosophy is based on health of mind, body and spirit, and in the early 1900s, the club built houses and cottages along the highway and oceanfront, which it rented out to its members. Its beachfront cottages offered members peace and beauty, conducive to rest and relaxation. Later, the houses and cottages were offered to nonmembers for low rent. The low rents attracted artists, surfers and the hippie lifestyle in the 1960s, which gave the area a bohemian-lifestyle reputation. Houses along the highway and beachfront cottages are long gone, including one of the area's longtime institutions, Topanga Ranch Market. In 2003, the Topanga Ranch Market, a business located off Pacific Coast Highway that had served the community and tourists since the 1950s, was demolished when California State Parks purchased the land from a parent company of the Los Angeles Athletic Club.

Topanga Beach and Topanga Canyon

Winding road signs are common sights along Pacific Coast Highway, particularly north of Malibu, where the highway winds, climbs and drops in many sections. The stretch of highway from Malibu to Santa Monica is less challenging, except that it is often heavily congested with traffic and plagued with road repairs due to seasonal landslides and mudslides. Roads leading up to the canyons can be winding and challenging. The highway was basically carved out of the mountains and cliffs, making it susceptible to landfalls triggered by heavy rainfall, earthquakes and the like.

Topanga Beach is located off Pacific Coast Highway, west of Topanga Canyon Boulevard. The beach lies at the outlet of Topanga Creek, bordering Malibu to the north and Will Rogers State Beach to the south. Topanga Beach is a south-facing beach and is divided by Topanga Creek where it empties into the ocean. The beach west of the creek is Topanga, and South Topanga is east of the creek. Comprising a narrow stretch of sandy beach that is great for sunbathing, Topanga Beach is popular for visible marine life in its rocky areas, surfing, kayaking, swimming and fishing. The beach is a great vantage point for Santa Monica Bay and Catalina Island.

In the mid-1900s, Hollywood celebrities who made Lower Topanga Canyon their home included Humphrey Bogart, Peter Lorre, Carole Lombard, Shirley Temple and Ida Lupino, to name only a few. Its history of beach surfing, together with its lively canyon residents in the Santa Monica Mountains, dates back to the 1950s, and it was well known as a "hip" community. Its beach was considered somewhat private because houses along the highway shielded it from the public, making its access difficult. In the 1960s, the beachfront cottages were mostly occupied by surfers, writers and artists, among others, who all shared a love of the ocean.

Located in the Santa Monica Mountains, Topanga Canyon comprises lands of Topanga State Park and Santa Monica Mountains Conservancy and is part of the Santa Monica Mountains National Recreation Area. Topanga Canyon was a popular weekend spot for celebrities in the 1920s because the seclusion of the canyon offered privacy, serenity and a natural, organic atmosphere seemingly far

Neighboring Topanga is Pacific Palisades, where a large landslide occured on Pacific Coast Highway on April 5, 1983. Landslides along coastal areas are common, some being small and easily unnoticed. Small rocks and dirt that are often seen at the base of a hill and along the side of the road can be a precursor to a larger slide. Sudden heavy rain, wind or an earthquake could trigger a weakened hillside, causing extensive damage to or destruction of structures below it, vehicles passing by it and the road below it. *Copyright 1983, California Department of Transportation.*

Completion of the hillside reinforcement project along Pacific Coast Highway on December 1, 1933. The project took a year to complete. Methods used to prevent and reduce landslides included the installation of corrugated metal pipe culverts, perforated metal pipe underdrains and spillway assemblies, constructing slope ditches, utilization of riprap (concrete rubble) and installation of laminated timber guardrails on timber posts. *Copyright 1933, California Department of Transportation.*

away from the hustle and bustle of the nearby city. In addition to many UFO sightings in the canyon through the years, artists, songwriters and musicians developed some of their well-known works while living in the canyon. The canyon was also home to a popular nudist club for several decades. Abundant with coyotes, mule deer, bobcats, raccoons, skunks, snakes and a rainbow of birds, nature enthusiasts, mountain bikers, hikers and equestrians find the canyon to be a great nearby retreat.

Despite natural disasters, which include fire, earthquake, flood and mud-, land- and rockslides, many coastal residents stand their ground and battle the elements, rebuilding in many cases. Topanga Creek is known for its occasional flooding, causing severe and extensive road erosion. Landslides are widespread and occur all over the country, especially around coastal areas, causing billions of dollars in damages and the loss of lives. Landslides commonly occur when other events, such as earthquakes, fires and floods, set them in motion. Although gravity is the force that enables landslides, it is the disruption of the land that triggers a landslide. On an incline, when the friction between sediment cover and underlying bedrock is disrupted, gravity will overcome the force of friction, resulting in a landslide. Water reduces the friction between bedrock and overlying sediment, which accounts for landslides along the coast after rainstorms. Similarly, if the vibration of the earth's crust in an earthquake is strong enough to disrupt the force of friction that holds sediments in place on a hillside, it can result in a landslide. Fire is a great threat in the canyon because of the canyon's abundance of majestic coast live oaks, California sycamores and grasses. More importantly, the roots of trees and plants help stabilize soil on an incline, but when fire strikes and the plants are lost, the razed area is susceptible to a landslide. One of the more devastating fires in the area is known as the "Old Topanga Fire." Occurring in 1993, the fire took ten days to fully extinguish and burned one thousand acres and over three hundred structures.

Los Angeles County's coast, particularly from Malibu to Pacific Palisades, is rugged and steep because of a continuing uplift of the Santa Monica Mountains. The heavily traveled stretch of highway beneath the mountains and hills is often significantly affected by winter storms that cause shoreline erosion, and development of urban and recreational tracts into hillsides and cliffs creates further potential for landslides.

Founded by Will Geer, the Will Geer Theatricum Botanicum was opened as a place for victimized actors and folk singers of the McCarthy-era blacklisting to perform. The theater was popular for its plays and concerts. After Will Geer's death in 1978, the theater began to transform into a professional repertory that incorporates educational programs and musical events. The theater has been honored with the prestigious Margaret Harford Award for Sustained Excellence in Theater from the Los Angeles Drama Critics Circle, and its artistic director, Ellen Geer, was bestowed the LA Weekly Career Achievement Award. *Theatricum Botanicum.*

Historical Landmarks and Points of Interest

One of the canyon's popular attractions is the Theatricum Botanicum, a 299-seat outdoor amphitheater located in an area that has been dubbed the "artists' colony," founded by Will Geer (1902–1978), an American actor best known for his role as Zeb Walton, or "Grandpa," on the television series *The Waltons* (1971–1981). Will Geer was blacklisted in the 1950s during the McCarthy era, in which he was accused of being a Communist. It was then that he moved to Topanga and opened the Theatricum Botanicum.

Traveling inland from Pacific Coast Highway on Sunset Boulevard to Los Liones Drive, there are several trails that will lead to the Backbone Trail. Topanga State Park offers thirty-six miles of trails with vantage points of the Pacific Ocean. Located between Pacific Palisades to the south, Topanga Canyon to the west and Rustic Canyon to the east, it is a mine of geological formations, earthquake faults, marine fossils, volcanic intrusions and sedimentary formations. There are many small streams and creeks that support native fish and some endangered fish, such as southern steelhead trout and western pond turtles. The park is considered to be the world's largest wild land situated within the boundaries of a large city. This might account for the many UFO sightings that are typically reported from remote wild land areas. The Los Angeles County Board of Supervisors is in favor of designating a portion of Topanga Canyon Boulevard as a state scenic highway because of the thousands of visitors who annually travel it. It is one of the county's most scenic mountain highways and stretches from the Santa Monica Mountains' foothills of the San Fernando Valley down to Pacific Coast Highway and the ocean.

Today, Topanga is still known as a bohemian-type community with artists, musicians, writers and nature enthusiasts composing many of its residents. The community offers the public a taste of its flavors in annual events, such as Topanga Days (Memorial Day Weekend), Topanga Earth Day, Topanga Canyon Artists' Studio Tour and music festivals. Its "mountains to the sea" enclave is one of Los Angeles's must-see unique and eclectic communities, whether you simply drive by its part of the ocean on Pacific Coast Highway or take a turn off the highway onto Topanga Canyon's steep, winding, scenic boulevard.

Chapter 3

Pacific Palisades and Will Rogers State Beach

The word "palisade" refers to a wall or fence that is made from wooden stakes or tree trunks. Different countries in early eras built palisades in different ways and for different reasons. The Greeks and Romans built palisades to protect their military camps, and in South Africa, palisades were constructed to deter crime by surrounding houses with perimeter defenses. The main purpose of a palisade is to protect something, allowing the protected thing to be set apart and kept safe from a threat.

Majestically situated between Topanga and Santa Monica above Pacific Coast Highway is the beautiful Pacific Palisades. Perched atop cliffs overlooking the Pacific Ocean, it is primarily a residential community and has been a popular area among Angelenos, especially Hollywood celebrities, dating as far back as the 1920s when Sunset Boulevard was extended down to the beach at Pacific Coast Highway.

In 1822, a group of people met in Temescal Canyon to select individual lots from a tract they had jointly purchased. The canyon was full of oak trees, one of which they named Founder's Oak. It marked the day of their meeting and the beginning of what would later become Pacific Palisades. Its early history has roots in filmmaking. American silent film director, producer and actor Thomas Ince (1882–1924) created a western film factory in 1911. Ince employed hundreds of people, many of whom lived and settled in the area. Later, Reverend

Roosevelt Highway in 1938, taken north of Santa Monica. A four-lane highway constructed of asphalt, Roosevelt Highway was one of several early names the coastal highway has had throughout the years. It was once listed as Legislative Route 60, then Route 1 and then U.S. 101A, but despite its many names, Route 1 became its official designated name, widely known as Pacific Coast Highway. The beachside land that joins the highway shows significant erosion, as well as an unprotected hillside above the highway. *Copyright January 8, 1939, California Department of Transportation.*

Charles H. Scott and the Southern California Methodist Episcopal Church purchased hilltop land and founded Pacific Palisades.

Beginning in the 1930s and continuing for more than a decade, a German and Austrian community began to grow in Pacific Palisades and nearby Brentwood, an affluent community bordering Pacific Palisades, as a result of their exile from Nazi Germany. The European

A mountain hillside above Pacific Coast Highway is contracted to be reinforced as a measure to prevent a landslide. The photo was taken on February 1, 1933, before construction. Slope excavations were mostly done with tractors and bulldozers. Material was excavated and pushed down the existing slopes by bulldozers and then picked up by power shovels and loaded into dump trucks or dumped in the ocean. *Copyright 1933, California Department of Transportation.*

community largely comprised writers, artists and intellectuals. Although their residency in the area was temporary, some created legendary works that will remain forever, including Theodor Adorno and Max Horkheimer's *Dialectic of Enlightenment*, Berthold Brecht's

Galileo, Thomas Mann's *Dr. Faustus* and Arnold Schoenberg's *Moses and Aaron*. When the war ended, both Adorno and Horkheimer returned to Germany and Mann to Switzerland. The area has long been home to many notables, including California's former governor Arnold Schwarzenegger, who lived in the community for several years.

In the 1990s, California—especially its coastal communities—was hit hard by the El Niño storms, causing several mudslides and landslides of earth and rocks, which resulted in the closing of large portions of Pacific Coast Highway. Landslides are an ongoing concern and one of the highway's biggest problems, forcing Caltrans crews to remove dirt and debris, excavate unstable portions of bluffs, install drainage pipes and relandscape hillside areas. In 1958, a landslide spilled onto Pacific Coast Highway in Pacific Palisades, which forced the closure of long sections of the highway. A landslide affecting the highway is always devastating not only because of the damage it causes but also because of the traffic congestion it creates on Pacific Coast Highway and nearby roads that intersect with the highway. It is unknown whether the potential of frequent and devastating landslides, coastal erosion and corrosion and the cost of its maintenance were considered during the planning of a highway that would run through mountains.

Inasmuch as erosion is part of the rock cycle, the coastal landscape is formed by erosion and is constantly changing. Weather—water, temperature and wind—is the main cause of erosion. Acid rain can dissolve rocks, as can pounding waves, rushing water, leaching groundwater and floods. It's bad enough that nature on its own can cause a landslide, but exacerbating the process is urban development, making it no surprise that a highway constructed between land and sea takes the brunt of the blows.

A landslide is a term used to describe any type of downhill movement of rock, mud, soil or snow. Mudslides are typically caused by sudden heavy rains and consist of soil, water and debris, and an avalanche is usually related to snow, which we don't have to worry about in Southern California. But a slide is a slide, whether it is rock or mud, and they can be equally devastating and just as destructive. It is not uncommon along this stretch of highway in Pacific Palisades for a landslide to blanket portions of the road with dirt, rocks and debris, forcing its closure until the debris is removed and the installation of K-rails or concrete to keep dirt and rocks off the highway.

Ongoing efforts include the use of different methods of landslide prevention, such as the excavation of unstable portions of bluffs,

A landslide on May 5, 1958, shows the massive loss of earth under a large section of Pacific Coast Highway in Pacific Palisades. The coastal highway was largely carved out of mountains, hills and cliffs. Such areas are naturally weakened by storms, flooding and corrosion from salt water. The highway is constantly being repaired due to earth movement, heavy rains, storms and erosion. *Copyright 1958, California Department of Transportation.*

demolishing of ridgetop homes, construction of storm drain systems, landscaping and grading hillsides to deter erosion and removal of rocks along slopes that could roll onto the highway. Removal of rocks from the face of slopes is sometimes done manually, using picks, shovels, pry bars and rope. In some cases, slope stabilization is necessary due to heavy rains forming rock "ledges." Removal of rock ledges is necessary if they pose a threat of breaking off, causing a landslide. The use of heavy equipment, such as a thirty-foot-long-reach excavator, are used to remove slide material, and larger long-reach excavators are used for more complex and delicate areas because every hill, bluff or mountain is unique, which makes them inherently unpredictable.

In his article "The Long and Winding Road," Matthew W. Roth, Auto Club historian, wrote:

This photo shows another angle of the mountain hillside after the reinforcement project along Pacific Coast Highway on December 1, 1933. Several methods continue to be used in preventing landslides and mudslides, but the location of the highway on a narrow strip of land between mountains and the ocean makes it almost impossible to keep it clear of earth debris. *Copyright 1933, California Department of Transportation.*

> *The engineers' appreciation for resculpting nature developed into full and unapologetic expression during the course of the giant project. In 1929, when they declared the coast road complete, they did not dwell on such prosaic matters as connecting county seats, relieving congestion, or the road's ability to enrich frontage owners. They focused instead on the "magnificent new highway, its scenic setting along the sea, and the beaches and cliffs that adorn it."*

Pacific Palisades's coast is rugged and steep, but despite its precarious location and conditions—prone to fires, mudslides and landslides—it remains one of the city's most desirable areas to live.

Temescal Canyon Park is located inland off Pacific Coast Highway and is a great location to access hiking trails. Will Rogers State Historic Park and Polo Club has been designated as a historical preservation site and is open to the public for viewing and is the last remaining polo ground in the county. The site was once the ranch home of actor Will Rogers (1879–1935), who is best known as an American actor, vaudeville performer, humorist and cowboy. In the 1920s, Rogers purchased the land and developed a ranch along the coast. He owned

186 acres of what is now primarily Pacific Palisades. After the death of his wife, Betty, in 1944, the ranch was converted into a state park. Will Rogers State Beach is off Pacific Coast Highway and located on the Santa Monica Bay. The beach runs along Pacific Coast Highway from Topanga Canyon Boulevard to Santa Monica. It is a popular local beach for surfing, volleyball, gymnastics and its children's playground and is part of the South Bay Bicycle Trail. A portion of its beach is unofficially named "Ginger Rogers Beach" by the gay community, dating back to the 1950s, and is located between Temescal Canyon Park and Santa Monica Beach.

Historical Landmarks and Points of Interest

In the 1920s, Castle Rock, a nearly fifty-foot rock, was located on the beach between Pacific Palisades and Santa Monica. It was a popular landmark for tourists and locals and frequently featured on postcards and used as a backdrop in many films. It was blasted away in 1945 by 350 pounds of dynamite to make way for the widening of the highway.

The lighthouse next to Pacific Coast Highway was erected in the early 1900s and marked the site of Long Wharf located at Portero Canyon. It was located around one half mile north of Santa Monica. The lighthouse was the lifeguard headquarters for Will Rogers State Beach. Plans to save the lighthouse and relocate it to the Pepperdine University campus in Malibu failed in 1972, when the tower was unable to survive the attempted removal. *Copyright California Department of Transportation.*

Because of the rock's popularity, engineers preserved the base of the rock by constructing a turnout on its flat top as a beach vantage point.

Another notable attraction easily accessible off Pacific Coast Highway is the Self-Realization Fellowship Lake Shrine at Sunset, founded in 1950 by Paramahansa Yogananda (1893–1952). Paramahansa Yogananda, best known for his book *Autobiography of a Yogi*, was the famous Indian yogi and guru who brought the teachings of meditation and Kriya Yoga to millions of westerners.

Perched atop a hill above Pacific Coast Highway in Pacific Palisades is the Getty Villa. The Getty Villa is one of two locations of the J. Paul Getty Museum. The Getty Villa opened in 1974 and has a collection of over forty thousand Greek, Roman and Etruscan antiquities. It is no wonder why industrialist and oil magnate J. Paul Getty (1892–1976) chose the site to build a re-creation of Villa dei Papiri in Herculaneum, a first-century Roman country house. Enveloped in peaceful and beautiful landscape of colorful bougainvillea, eucalyptus and pine trees overlooking the ocean, it was a prime location, as it still is today. The area surrounding the Getty Villa is called Castellammare, and its neighborhood streets bear Italian names. It's as close to Pompeii as you're going to get in Los Angeles.

Chapter 4
Santa Monica

Pacific Coast Highway takes a detour near the famous Santa Monica Pier, turning inland from Santa Monica at I-10 East (Santa Monica Freeway) to Lincoln Boulevard, also known as Pacific Coast Highway 1. This junction is one of the busiest and most heavily congested stretches of Pacific Coast Highway in Southern California. Traffic congestion in the area dates back to the 1920s when autos and horse buggies traveled the road, but traffic today is caused by I-10 West coming into Santa Monica's coastal area through the McClure Tunnel, street traffic coming down onto Pacific Coast Highway north from Ocean Avenue and traffic from Lincoln Boulevard. Its stretch of highway is also one of the most troublesome landslide areas, which sometimes forces highway closures. Lincoln Boulevard (Pacific Coast Highway 1) runs closest to the coast, passing through the neighborhoods of Venice Beach, Marina del Rey, Playa Vista and Westchester. Lincoln Boulevard then becomes south Sepulveda Boulevard, also known as Pacific Coast Highway 1. Sepulveda Boulevard continues past Los Angeles International Airport (LAX) and into the South Bay communities.

The history of Pacific Coast Highway in Santa Monica plays a significant role in the city's growth dating back to the early 1900s. The highway was once named Roosevelt Highway, which opened in the early 1920s and created a route from Ventura to Santa Monica. It later became California State Route 1 in 1964, commonly referred to as Pacific Coast Highway but still locally referred to as Palisades Beach Road. Santa Monica and its beach are widely known as one of Los Angeles's popular tourist destinations that is worth the wait and traffic delays that are part and parcel of Los Angeles's popular coastal communities.

Santa Monica's early history dates back to the Portola Expedition in the 1700s and the era of land grants after Mexico won its independence from Spain. Don Francisco Sepulveda was granted provisional title to Rancho San Vicente y Santa Monica in 1828, which he used for cattle and sheep grazing; and a provisional title was given to Ysidro Reyes and Francisco Marquez for the Boca de Santa Monica Rancho, which was later confirmed by Governor Alvarado in 1939, located in the Santa Monica Canyon. After California became a state in 1850, Colonel Robert S. Baker (1826–1894) purchased Rancho San Vicente y Santa Monica in 1872, and in 1874, U.S. senator John P. Jones (1829–1912) of Nevada purchased a three-fourths interest in Colonel Baker's ranch.

By 1876, the Southern Pacific Railroad had a rail line that ran from San Francisco to Los Angeles. Both embraced a vision of Santa Monica becoming the Los Angeles port. The Long Wharf opened in 1893 and served the Los Angeles shipping industry, and a Southern Pacific train transported goods from the Long Wharf. However, when Santa Monica was not chosen to be Los Angeles's main port in 1908, service to the wharf was discontinued, and it was eventually dismantled. The Southern Pacific train tracks were later removed to create a portion of the Roosevelt Highway, which later became Route 1. Turning its vision from becoming a main port and harbor city, it focused on its beautiful assets—canyon, springs, streams, beach and city overlooking the ocean. Santa Monica grew to become a popular and frequently visited resort for the wealthy, who named it the "Gold Coast."

In the early years, many of its residents were Hollywood celebrities, including actress Marion Davies, whose estate on the beachfront was built for her in the 1920s by William Randolph Hearst (1863–1951) and is located on Pacific Coast Highway. It was considered the most extravagant home along the Gold Coast, consisting of five acres. The estate was later sold and converted into a hotel and health club. In 1960, the state purchased the property and leased it to the City of Santa Monica. Some of the early Hollywood celebrities who lived along the Gold Coast included Mary Pickford and her husband, Douglas Fairbanks; Norma Shearer; Merle Oberon; Paulette Goddard; and Louis B. Mayer. Santa Monica Beach was prized for its resort atmosphere because it lacked the busy, commercial and industrialized landscape of the Port of Los Angeles in San Pedro. By the 1920s, Santa Monica was a thriving city and had a twenty-passenger electric tram service that was located south of Santa Monica Pier and ran along the Ocean Front Promenade between Ocean Park and Looff Pier.

The construction of the Roosevelt Highway along Santa Monica's coast is interwoven with the history of the city's growth. Cliffs along the coast were scaled back in order to create a dirt road that would link Ocean Avenue to the Roosevelt Highway. The dirt road was mainly used by pedestrians for easy access to the beach. Today, the road is made of old concrete paving and called the California Incline, a heavily traveled road that links Ocean Avenue to north Route 1 and marks the beginning of the detour that takes Route 1 south away from the coastline.

The city's high bluffs separate its northern side from the beaches. The famous U.S. Route 66, known as the Main Street of America or the Mother Road, is one of America's most famous roads. It originally ran from Chicago, Illinois, to California, covering 2,448 miles, and it ended in Santa Monica. Up the California Incline along Ocean Avenue at Palisades Park, which sits atop a bluff overlooking Pacific Coast Highway and the ocean, is a commemorative brass plaque marking the official end of Route 66 (even though the California Route 66 Preservation Foundation says Route 66 officially ends when it merges at the intersection of Lincoln and Olympic Boulevards). In 2009, the Santa Monica Pier was officially designated as the West Coast's terminus to Route 66. The sign pays tribute to the original sign that overlooked the Santa Monica Pier in the 1930s, which has long since vanished.

Santa Monica Pier

One of the most noted attractions at the Santa Monica Pier is the Looff Hippodrome, listed on the National Register of Historic Places

Designated as the official western terminus of the famous Route 66 (length of Route 66 from Chicago to Santa Monica), the Santa Monica Pier is (or is believed to be) the West Coast's end to Route 66. A replica of a lost "End of the Trail" sign that once stood on the Santa Monica Pier in the 1930s was unveiled in a ceremony at the landmark during the pier's centennial in 2009. *Photo by Mikhail Kolesnikov.*

The Santa Monica Pier is a double-jointed pier, comprising two separate piers. The long, narrow municipal pier was constructed in 1909 for the purpose of transporting sewer pipes beyond the breakers. The short, wider pier, known as the "Pleasure Pier," was constructed in 1916 by Charles I.D. Looff, a renowned carousel maker from New York. Looff created an amusement park that was partly built on beachfront property with the western half on a pier. The park features a carousel, a small roller coaster and a large Ferris wheel. Looff also constructed a hippodrome building, which is listed on the National Register of Historic Places. The white hippodrome can be seen east of the pier at the entrance, resembling an upside-down funnel. *Jon B. Lovelace Collection of California Photographs.*

in Los Angeles County. In ancient Greece, a hippodrome was an open-air stadium with an oval course for horse and chariot races or an arena for equestrian shows. In Santa Monica, the Looff Hippodrome is a structure located at the shore end of the pier that houses a carousel built by Charles Looff (1852–1918), a master carver and builder of hand-carved carousels and amusement rides. Looff built Coney Island's first carousel in 1876 and is credited for having built over fifty carousels during his lifetime. In 1916, Looff and his son designed and built a wide but shorter pleasure park along the south side of the 1,600-foot-long municipal pier, which was built in 1909 for the purpose of running treated sewage out to the ocean. The second pier was named the Looff Pier, and together it created a double-jointed

pier. The Looff Pier was an amusement pier with a hippodrome and carousel, a Blue Streak Racer wooden roller coaster and the Whip and the Aeroscope thrill rides.

In 1924, the Looff family sold the pleasure park to the Santa Monica Amusement Company, which upgraded the roller coaster with the Whirlwind Dipper and added a fifteen-thousand-square-foot La Monica Ballroom. In 1934, a breakwater was constructed, and the Santa Monica Yacht Harbor was born. The neon sign installed at the entrance of the pier in 1940 still stands today, even though there

Aerial view of Santa Monica's double-jointed pier, showing the long, narrow municipal pier that extends beyond the Pleasure Pier. The end of the municipal pier has been a popular fishing area for decades. When Walter Newcomb purchased the Pleasure Pier from the Looff family in 1943, it became the Newcomb Pier. Today, the Newcomb Pier is called Pacific Park, which opened in 1996 as a free-admission amusement park. *Jon B. Lovelace Collection of California Photographs.*

hasn't been a yacht in its harbor for over forty years. In 1943, Walter Newcomb purchased the Santa Monica Amusement Company's lease of the pleasure park, which became the Newcomb Pier. The history of the pier's ebbs and flows has made the double-jointed pier even stronger as years passed. Today, it is called Pacific Park, one of Los Angeles's main coastal attractions, and is Santa Monica's most popular landmark. The large crowd of visitors accounts for the significant amount of traffic congestion on the Pacific Coast Highway stretch in Santa Monica.

Widely known by its famous neon sign at the entrance to the pier, it's been the trademark and icon of both the pier and the city of Santa Monica since it was installed in 1940. In celebration of the pier's newly built concrete ramp, the neon sign was erected by the Santa Monica Pier Businessmen's Association. In the 1930s, Santa Monica was a growing boat harbor. Yachts, fishing boats and a cruise liner to Catalina filled its harbor until the 1960s, when its breakwater began to sink and boating activities in Santa Monica began to significantly decline. *Jon B. Lovelace Collection of California Photographs.*

Santa Monica Beach and Santa Monica Canyon

Located on Pacific Coast Highway, Santa Monica Beach has over three miles of coastline and is popular for its palm trees that frame the landscape. Its water, sand and land activities include swimming, surfing, fishing, beach volleyball (before it became an Olympic sport), chess and biking along its paved bike path from Will Rogers State Beach to neighboring Venice Beach and Marina del Rey. The popularity of Santa Monica Beach dates back to the 1800s, when the Arcadia Hotel opened in 1887 and became a popular getaway resort. The hotel was considered one of the most prestigious hotels along the Pacific Coast and attracted the rich and famous. The North Beach Bathhouse was built in 1894 and was popular for its hot saltwater baths, restaurant and bowling pavilion. A walkway that connected Ocean Park Piers and the Santa Monica Pier was a heavy foot-traffic route. Exclusive beach clubs were built along the oceanfront in the 1920s, which included the Santa Monica Athletic Club, a swimming club, the Deauville, Beach

Club, Wavecrest, Edgewater, Breakers, Casa del Mar and Sea Breeze (later the Jonathan Club). Bicycle races were held along Pacific Coast Highway, and beauty contests were held on the beach and were one of its more popular events. The famous Muscle Beach was originally located on Santa Monica Beach in the 1930s, despite it not being an officially designated beach. It began with a group of men gathering to perform gymnastics and weightlifting on the beach, including well-known names such as Jack LaLanne and Steve "Hercules" Reeves. It soon became known as the showplace of musclemen and later included women and children displaying agility and physical strength. Participants performed solo, as a duo or in groups, and the displays soon gained international fame. Crowds of people would gather to watch the demonstrations for entertainment. However, Santa Monica became concerned about the type of people the demonstrations were attracting, especially during the Depression years, when many were out of work and flocked to the beach as a source of free entertainment. Santa Monica was striving to maintain its reputation as a resort community, and the crowd at Muscle Beach was beginning to cast a shadow on it. Santa Monica decided to remove the equipment and staging platforms to prevent continuation of the events on its beach. That marked the end of Muscle Beach in Santa Monica. Muscle Beach became the new attraction at neighboring Venice Beach and continues its display of weightlifting today.

The Santa Monica Canyon comprises an area shaped by three watersheds and includes lower Rustic Canyon and lower Sullivan Canyon. Populated with oak and sycamore trees and natural springs, Santa Monica and its canyon came to be regarded as a resort community. In the early years, celebrities and the wealthy class found the canyon to be a quiet and serene place to live.

Despite their rocky appearance, Santa Monica's unstable bluffs are an ancient sand dune and river plain and through the years have been a big problem for the highway below it. Several methods of controlling its deterioration include installation of horizontal drainage pipes—called hydraugers, which collect groundwater—surface treatments utilizing native plants, application of sprayed chemical grout and removal of overhanging soil blocks and old pavement. Preserving the bluffs' natural appearance is factored into the methods used to prevent the destruction of their natural formation. The Northridge earthquake of 1994 caused several sections of the bluff to fall onto Pacific Coast Highway. The bluffs' cliff face has disappeared over the years by small

In addition to netting hillsides and cliffs along Pacific Coast Highway, barrier walls are also constructed at the foot of the hill to shield the road and traffic from mud and rock debris. The netting and barrier walls are constructed to withstand several thousand pounds of rock from breaking through the net. The photo shows a portion of a vulnerable hillside with significant erosion. It has been netted and a barrier wall constructed at its foot. *John Moss Photography*.

An original sloped mountain hillside above Pacific Coast Highway in need of reinforcement to prevent landslides. Uneven dirt and rock can be seen, as well as hillside erosion. Dirt and rock have fallen onto the highway, and a small guard wall was erected to aid in preventing dirt and mud from spilling onto the highway. The contract date to begin construction was December 30, 1932. *Copyright 1932, California Department of Transportation.*

Opposite, bottom: Looking north from Santa Monica at Pacific Coast Highway in the early 1930s when it was designated as Route 60. Significant erosion can be seen in the bluffs and hillsides that span the distance from Santa Monica to Pacific Palisades and beyond. The beachside land that joins the highway also appears weak, unlike the reinforced sea barrier of rocks and boulders protecting the lighthouse in the distance. Sea barriers and seawalls may cause erosion of nearby unprotected coastal areas. *Copyright 1930, California Department of Transportation.*

pieces falling from it over time, as well as from significant landslides. Water is the bluffs' worst enemy. The California coast differs from the Atlantic and Gulf Coasts due to the type of storms that hit the West Coast and its topography. Coastal flooding along California's coast is typically from high tides, storm surges and high-wave energy. During El Niño, storms follow a southerly path that results in intense rainfall and high tides along the coastline, resulting in flooding and coastal erosion.

Netting used on hillsides along the coast has helped keep falling debris off the highway. Santa Monica's bluffs have had more than thirty landslides since 1930, which evidences their instability in general and that of Palisades Park, which sits on them, in particular. The City of

Santa Monica dearly regards its bluffs as much as California regards its coastal highway, which results in huge monetary expenditures to keep an impractical, unstable and high-maintenance thing in existence. As a native Californian with a fond attachment to Pacific Coast Highway and childhood memories of times spent at Palisades Park, I, too, share the desire to keep these two impractical marvels.

Netting hillsides and cliffs along Pacific Coast Highway is a significant method of keeping landslides and rockslides from falling onto the highway, keeping the road safe from debris and damage and traffic on the highway. The process involves anchors inserted along the brow of the hillside or cliff before a helicopter is used to drape the net over the area. The nets are then fastened to the anchors, which act as solid protective units and cover. *John Moss Photo.*

Landmarks and Points of Interest

Santa Monica's Third Street Promenade is a popular shopping area with restaurants, novelty shops and theaters. Located in the downtown area and in close distance to the beach, it is always bustling with visitors and locals. The Bergamot Station is a warehouse that holds art galleries, the Santa Monica Museum of Art and unique shops. Montana Avenue consists of ten blocks of more than one hundred unique upscale shops. Ocean Avenue, located at the north end of Santa Monica and stretching to Pico Boulevard, runs parallel to Palisades Park. The Palisades Park bluffs overlook Pacific Coast Highway, the Santa Monica Pier and Santa Monica State Beach.

Chapter 5
Venice Beach and Marina del Rey

Continuing south on Pacific Coast Highway, the coastal road splits into Interstate 10 East (Santa Monica Freeway) and Route 1/Lincoln Boulevard South, passing through the coastal neighborhoods of Venice Beach, Marina del Rey, Playa Vista and Westchester.

Ocean Park

Santa Monica and South Santa Monica (Ocean Park/Venice) are closely connected in history. The communities were both settled in the 1870s, with only a gully separating them. Ocean Park was developed by Abbot Kinney (1850–1920) beginning in the late 1800s and into the early 1900s. Kinney's business, Ocean Park Development Company, built roads, homes, parks and piers, which attracted many people to the newly developed area. Kinney envisioned Ocean Park to become a "Venice of America" community and began constructing Venetian-style buildings and water canals. Converting 160 acres of flatland into residential subdivisions, he constructed roads, waterways, canals and bridges that resembled Venice, Italy, including gondola rides in its canals. Ocean Park became one of Los Angeles's most unique and popular communities to live in and visit, but its life was short-lived. When the newness of its grandeur waned and the expense of its maintenance increased, "Venice of America" declined, and its canals were drained and buried with dirt.

PANORAMIC VIEW
OF OCEAN PARK, CAL.
COPYRIGHT 1914, BY GEO. RICE & SONS

Ocean Park dates back to the early 1900s when Abott Kinney envisioned the area becoming the "Venice of America." He constructed homes, buildings, canals, parks and piers that resembled Venice, Italy. The area became the pleasure pier/park capital of the West Coast, but when the novelty waned and the Great Depression hit, the grand "Venice of America" began to disappear. Today, its canals and pleasure piers are gone, leaving a few remnants of old structures and only part of its name, Venice Beach. *Jon B. Lovelace Collection of California Photographs.*

The Kinney Pier was once a 1,200-foot-long pleasure pier built in the early 1900s in Venice Beach. It had an auditorium, a ship restaurant, a dance hall, a hot saltwater plunge and a long stretch of Venetian-style buildings that housed several arcades. By 1910, a Venice Scenic Railway, an aquarium, a Virginia Reel, a racing derby, carnival rides and game booths were added. Another big attraction was its mile-long beach, which offered cottages and tents for rent. *Jon B. Lovelace Collection of California Photographs.*

Kinney's 1,200-foot-long pleasure pier, designed with Venetian-style structures and themes, had an auditorium, a ship restaurant, a dance hall and arcades. Its saltwater plunge, cottages and housekeeping tents were big attractions that brought people to its mile-long beach. After the Venice Scenic Railway, the Virginia Reel, the Whip, the racing derby, the aquarium, the rides and game booths were added, the pleasure pier was transformed into an amusement park. Plagued by storms and fire, the pier saw repeated destruction. Other piers in Ocean Park included Pickering Pleasure Pier, Sunset Pier and Lick Pier, all of which competed with each other in attractions, amenities and grandness. To add to Ocean Park's fame, the Los Angeles Turf Club and CBS studios constructed a nautical-themed amusement park on twenty-eight acres of beachfront land. The amusement park opened in 1958 as Pacific Ocean Park (more commonly called "POP") and was popular for several years, standardizing the "pay-one-price admission ticket." The entrance to the park featured a display of Neptune's Kingdom, with an underwater diorama of artificial sea life, including turtles, sharks, manta rays and the like. Coca-Cola, Westinghouse and Union 76, among other large corporations, displayed their logos as advertisements to further the amusement park's success. Unfortunately, the park fell on financial difficulties, partly due to Santa Monica's Ocean Park urban renewal project that caused obstacles for visitors desiring to visit the park, as well as its competition with another theme park called Disneyland. Pacific Ocean Park closed its doors in 1967. This marked the end of the large pleasure parks in Ocean Park.

Venice Beach

Today, Venice Beach includes the beach and boardwalk that runs parallel to the beach. The Venice Beach community has its roots dating back to the Ocean Park era, when artists, poets, musicians and "beatniks" found a community atmosphere that promoted free expression. The community continues to be colored with bohemian-type residents and visitors who enjoy the eclectic, the colorful and the unconventional. This is not to imply in any way that Venice Beach as a whole is solely composed of what I just described. It is a community of people of similar minds, otherwise they would not live there or visit. Los Angeles is a melting pot of immigrants, and the city prides itself on its many cultures that have brought food, music, dance, festivals, celebrations and human enrichment to its neighbors. Many sections of the city are historically designated and populated with people and symbols of their chosen identity, such as Historic Filipinotown, Little Tokyo, Little Italy, Little Armenia and Thai Town, among others. West Hollywood is a predominately gay community, Silverlake is an upcoming trend-setting community and Venice Beach is just one of Los Angeles's many faceted communities.

Venice's history is filled with pleasure and amusement attractions, most of which have long since disappeared. The relocation of Muscle Beach to Venice Beach from Santa Monica dates back to the 1950s. In Venice, it was renamed Muscle Beach Venice California, or "the Pen." The display is situated on the boardwalk, also called Ocean Front Walk, north of the Venice Pier. Venice Beach is noted for its surf, largely as a result of the breakwater constructed during Kinney's development of Ocean Park.

Landmarks and Points of Interest

Canals, narrow streets, colorful murals and surrounding Venetian-style architecture are what make Venice Beach an eclectic and colorful bohemian-like neighborhood. Partial structures of the original buildings constructed during the early 1900s are still standing. Located along the southern portion of the beach is Venice Beach's 1,310-foot concrete fishing pier. Opening in 1964, it suffered damage in the 1983 El Niño storms and had to be closed, reopening in the 1990s. Venice Beach's breakwater is a popular surfing area for locals.

Marina del Rey

One of the largest man-made harbors, Marina del Rey is known for its small boats, dinghies and million-dollar yachts. The marina offers whale-watching trips, fishing excursions and charter rides to Catalina Island. The Waterfront is a public walkway where you can view the many boats docked or sailing in the marina. Mother's Beach is a popular nearby beach because of its calm water and amenities, which include playground equipment and volleyball nets. Fisherman's Village is designed to resemble a New England seaport. An upscale beach community, it is one of Los Angeles's prime residential areas.

Marina del Rey is a specially designed harbor with moorings for small boats and pleasure crafts, and it harbors over five thousand small-boat slips. Originally an area comprising wetlands, it was developed in the 1950s by the Army Corps of Engineers, funded and cooperatively planned by the federal government, Los Angeles County and private developers. Earlier plans to transform the marina into a commercial harbor for the City of Los Angeles lost out to San Pedro, as did Santa Monica. Its consolation was becoming the largest man-made marina in the country. Howard Hughes memorialized the marina with the construction of the Hughes Airport with a two-mile runway and the

An aerial view of Marina del Rey, located south of Venice Beach, off Lincoln Boulevard. It is the largest small craft harbor on the West Coast. Once known as Playa del Rey inlet, where the Los Angeles River emptied into the Pacific Ocean, the area was once mostly wetlands. When Santa Monica's Yacht Harbor breakwater began to weaken and sink, Marina del Rey's pleasure boat harbor that opened in 1965 began to grow in popularity. *Jon B. Lovelace Collection of California Photographs.*

building of the Hughes H-4 wooden aircraft/albatross, known as the legendary Spruce Goose.

Marina del Rey Beach

Today, Marina del Rey is landscaped with million-dollar homes, high-rise condominiums overlooking the marina, waterfront apartments, boat docks and manicured beach-sand playgrounds where beautiful people come out to play. It's an upscale beach community and is considered to be one of Los Angeles's most desired places in which to live.

Landmarks and Points of Interest

In the early 1950s, an eighty-acre amusement park named Hoppyland—after William Boyd (1895–1972), an actor known as Hopalong Cassidy—was a partner of the amusement park. The park closed around the mid-1950s due to the development of Marina del Rey. Today, the area's main attraction is its man-made marina. Shopping centers, retail stores and restaurants at Westside Beach and a visit to Fisherman's Village make for a nice weekend getaway or vacation. It's all there—concerts at Burton Park, gondola rides and bicycle and jogging paths—surrounded by serene seascapes.

Cattle grazing on flat lands and rolling hills along California's coast dates back to the early 1700s, when early Spanish missions were established from San Diego to Sonoma. After the Mexican war of independence from Spain in 1821, mission lands were typically granted or sold to former soldiers or their descendants for loyal service during the war. The lands became large ranchos, many comprising thousands of acres of land, which was ideal for cattle grazing. Ranchos produced cattle hides and tallow that boosted the state's economy. After the United States acquired California from Mexico under the Treaty of Guadalupe Hidalgo in 1848, which coincided with the California gold rush (1848–1855), hundreds of thousands of people flocked to California in search of gold, resulting in a large demand for beef. *Jon B. Lovelace Collection of California Photographs.*

An aerial view of Pacific Coast Highway running along the strip of land separating the Santa Monica Mountains from the Pacific Ocean. The coastal highway distance between Malibu and Santa Monica is around twenty-two miles of scenic landscape. Towering bluffs and looming hills at the edge of the road are part of the coastal highway's most scenic attractions, as well as its worst natural enemy. *Copyright California Department of Transportation.*

A lifeguard station at Zuma Beach during El Niño in the 1980s. Heavy rains caused flooding, mudslides and rockslides along Pacific Coast Highway. Large boulders and mud caused the closure of large sections of the highway. The highway along Los Angeles County's coast is sandwiched between hills and the Pacific Ocean. Heavy storms adversely affect the highway that is already prone to normal erosion, earth shifts and weakening hillsides. *John Moss Photography.*

Malibu Cove Colony is located off Pacific Coast Highway and south of Malibu Road. In the early 1920s, Hollywood celebrities began to lease lots and build vacation homes on the oceanfront land. The first celebrity to lease a lot was Swedish film actress Anna Q. Nilsson (1888–1974), and English actor Ronald Coleman (1891–1958) was the first celebrity to build a beach bungalow in the Colony. By the 1930s, the area boomed with many celebrities leasing and building cottages. *John Moss Photography*.

Opposite, bottom: The Malibu Lagoon is where Malibu Creek meets the Pacific Ocean. Fresh water flowing from the San Fernando Valley though the Santa Monica Mountains forms the canyon creek. In years past, the resulting lagoon provided fresh water to the Humaliwo village located south of the lagoon at Vaquero Point. Remnants of the Chumash village date back to the 1400s. Today, the lagoon is a state park and protected beach and is a resting spot for several species of migrating birds. *John Moss Photography*.

The beach at Malibu Cove Colony can be difficult to access because it is one of the most expensive beach communities on Pacific Coast Highway. Although there are no private beaches in California, other beaches that are more accessible off Pacific Coast Highway include Nicholas Canyon, Las Tunas, Lechuza, Escondido, Las Flores, La Costa, Latigo Point, Big Rock, Puerco, Ramirez Canyon (also known as Banning Harbor) and Corral Creek (one of the most photographed beaches). There is no denying that the main attraction of Malibu is its many beaches. *John Moss Photography*.

I get a fishing lesson from Malibu's "unofficial mayor," Lincoln Minor. Lincoln has been fishing off Malibu's pier for more than thirty years and is well known among locals who frequent the pier. Lincoln cheerfully provided me with a demonstration of his fishing tactics, stating that "it's also about using the right bait." In the 1970s, the pier offered sportfishing boat rides until its temporary closing in 1994, due to heavy rainstorms. *John Moss Photography*.

Originally founded and operating in Los Angeles, Pepperdine University relocated to the Malibu area after the Adamson family donated 130 acres to the school in 1968. Pepperdine broke ground in 1971 and reopened in its new location in the fall of 1972. The school today sits prominently on its 830 acres and is landscaped with a sea of manicured green grass. The university is one of Malibu's spectacular sites on Pacific Coast Highway. *John Moss Photography*.

Surfing Magazine featured John Moss surfing at Malibu Beach, known for being California's most famous right point break beach. Malibu's ideal surfing conditions attracted the likes of Tom Blake and Sam Reed, who are reported to have been the first to surf the area. Miki Dora, Angie Reno, Jay Riddle, Nathan Pratt, Skip Englom, Jeff Ho and Allen Sarlo, to name only a few, were soon to follow. *Courtesy of Peter "Doc" Brouillet*.

Sailboats grace the water at Malibu Beach. Southern California is known for its Mediterranean-type climate that is ideal for year-round sailing. During the summer months, average daytime temperatures range between the seventies and low eighties, and winter months are rarely too cold to not see a dozen or more boats sailing the coast. Popular sailing spots also include Marina del Rey, Santa Monica, Hermosa Beach, Redondo Beach, San Pedro and Long Beach. *John Moss Photography*.

Locals and tourists crowd the Santa Monica Pier. Easy access from the I-10, the California Incline and Pacific Coast Highway make a visit to the pier easy. A family-friendly place to visit, there is something for everyone. Pacific Park has a roller coaster, a Ferris wheel, an arcade and other rides. Restaurants, shops and kiosks sell food, shells and souvenirs. Fishing off the end of the pier has been a popular activity since the pier was built in 1909. *John Moss Photography*.

Perched on a hill overlooking Pacific Coast Highway, and sharing the border of Malibu and Pacific Palisades, is the Getty Villa. An education center and museum that is dedicated to the study of arts and cultures of ancient Greece, Rome and Etruria, its collection of antiquities dating from 6,500 BC to AD 400 is one of the most beautiful and educational places to visit just off the highway. *John Moss Photography.*

Stretching about three and a half miles from Will Rogers State Beach to Venice Beach, Santa Monica State Beach is a wide, sandy beach. A popular beach that is close to the city, it is where locals soak up the sun by sunbathing, playing volleyball, skating, biking, hiking and bodysurfing. The Santa Monica Pier and Pacific Park are seen in the background, as well as many sailboats in the harbor, most of which are from nearby Marina del Rey. *John Moss Photography*.

The California Incline connects Ocean Avenue with Pacific Coast Highway. Originally used as a walkway, called Sunset Trail, the Incline was constructed by cutting through the bluffs to allow pedestrians easy beach access in the late 1800s. The road Incline, comprising 1,400 feet, was constructed in 1930 and has become one of the city's most vital and traveled streets. *John Moss Photography*.

Opposite, bottom: An aerial view of Venice Beach showing its residential, commercial and beachfront neighborhood as it is today. It is most noted for its beach, canals and Ocean Front Walk, which comprises two and a half miles of pedestrian walkway. The walkway is heavily dotted with street performers, psychics, artists and an assortment of vendors selling items that range from unique crafts to sunglasses. Built up by Abbot Kinney in the early 1900s to resemble Venice, Italy, he called the area "Venice of America." *Carol Highsmith Archive Collection*.

Venice Boardwalk stretches around one and a half miles along the Pacific Ocean. Hundreds of vendors and performers line the boardwalk. Psychic readers, dancers, musicians, jugglers and artists offer entertainment and unique one-of-a-kind crafts and artistic creations. There's something on the boardwalk for everyone, including food. Junk food, carnival food, health food and medical marijuana dispensaries abound. It is one of Los Angeles County's most visited beaches because of its artistic and unusual flair. *John Moss Photography*.

Allen Sarlo, one of Malibu's most noted big-wave surfers, is seen surfing the waves at nearby Venice Beach in the 1980s. Dubbed the "Wave Killer" by the media, Sarlo surfed around the world on the pro circuit. In 1998, Sarlo made the cover of *Surfing Magazine*, showing a bottom turn on a twenty-plus-foot wave. The cover photo became one of the magazine's most memorable issues. Sarlo is one of many surfing greats of Southern California. *John Moss Photography.*

Hermosa Beach has two miles of sandy shoreline, which has been a popular South Bay beach for surfing and sunbathing dating back to the 1950s. Bicyclists, skaters, joggers and strollers take to the Strand, a paved walkway that runs along the beach. The original Hermosa Beach Municipal Pier was built in 1904 but was destroyed by storms in 1913. The rebuilt pier today is mainly used for fishing and as a scenic vantage point of the South Bay. *John Moss Photography*.

Dennis Jarvis, one of South Bay's most noted professional surfers, surfs the waves at Hermosa Beach in the 1980s. Jarvis created the Spyder Surfboard for high performance, and he used it to compete on the Professional World Tour. The Spyder Surfboard proved to be a success, and it soon became popular and widely in demand. Jarvis first opened Spyder Surf Shop at the corner of Artesia Boulevard and Pacific Coast Highway. In 1997, a second location opened on Hermosa Beach's Pier Plaza. *John Moss Photography*.

Hermosa Beach's sandy shoreline has been a favorite location for beach volleyball, a sport played by two teams consisting of two players on a sand court. Beach volleyball has been a popular sport on California's southern coast beaches since the game was reportedly first played on the sand at Santa Monica Beach. Although the first beach volleyball game was played at Santa Monica Beach, the first Hermosa Beach volleyball tournament was played with Ron Von Hagen and Henry Bergman, who won the title. *John Moss Photography*.

Opposite: Redondo Beach King Harbor is known for its small boats, paddle boats, paddleboarding and kayak anglers. King Harbor is a pleasure boat harbor operated by the City of Redondo Beach. Spotted bay bass, sand bass, calicos, bonitos, halibut and barracuda are some of the types of fish in the harbor, in addition to resident dolphins and sea lions. *John Moss Photography*.

Dennis Jarvis rides a six-foot wave at Redondo Beach during the Paradise Surfboard contest in the 1980s. A second surfer can be seen duck-diving into a wave. Jarvis was not only one of South Bay's great surfers, but he also proved to be a successful designer and creator of the Spyder Surfboard. Surfing competitions have been popular in the South Bay since 1962. Originally held at the Redondo Beach breakwater, it was discontinued in the early 1980s but soon moved to Hermosa Beach pier, where competitions are still held to this day. *John Moss Photography*.

Redondo Beach has had seven piers since 1889. Originally vying to become Los Angeles's main harbor, its early piers were constructed to receive and transport freight. After losing to San Pedro, piers were dismantled or destroyed by storms. New piers contructed were used as pleasure piers for fishermen and tourists, but they, too, suffered damage from storms. The Sportfishing Pier opened in 1970 and is still in use today. Redondo Beach's pier marks the seventh generation of restored piers constructed of reinforced concrete yet incorporating design features that are reminiscent of its earlier pier structures. *John Moss Photography*.

Opposite: Located on the western portion of Los Angeles County, and encompassing around twenty-one miles, Torrance borders Palos Verdes Peninsula on the south, Gardena on the north, Redondo Beach on both the north and west boundaries, Lomita on the east and the Pacific Ocean on the west. Pacific Coast Highway is a main vein that links many of the South Bay communities. Pacific Coast Highway runs east to west through Torrance's industrial and business centers. *Photo by John Stebbins*.

Located alongside a picturesque harbor, Long Beach is considered the second-busiest port in the country. The city's history is interwoven with the growth of its harbor. Activities began to bustle in the early 1900s, particularly by the opening of the Panama Canal in 1914, because both Long Beach and San Pedro ports were the closest to it. Construction of terminals, large corporations operating out of the harbor and U.S. Navy facilities were some of the activities in the harbor that opened thousands of jobs, leading to a boom in the city's growth. *John Moss Photography.*

Chapter 6
Sepulveda/El Segundo

California Route 1 continues through Playa del Rey and heads south toward Los Angeles International Airport (LAX) from Sepulveda Boulevard in the city of El Segundo. Playa del Rey is another small coastal community with sand dunes, also known as "the Bluffs." The dunes run along the coastline and south to Palos Verdes. Similar to Marina del Rey, its northern section was originally wetlands until the development of a concrete channel in Venice for Ballona Creek and the development of Marina del Rey.

Sepulveda Boulevard stretches nearly 42.8 miles from the north end of the San Fernando Valley to the Hermosa Beach city limits. It's named after the Sepulveda family, who were granted half of a Spanish land grant for Rancho San Pedro with Juan José Dominguez in 1784. Sepulveda Boulevard is a main thoroughfare through West Los Angeles, merging with Lincoln Boulevard on the north side of the Los Angeles International Airport before its transition into State Route 1, Pacific Coast Highway. Pacific Coast Highway continues under the airport's runway tunnel and into El Segundo.

In earlier years, El Segundo was part of Rancho Sausal Redondo, a land grant owned by Antonio Ygnacio Avila, which ran from Playa del Rey to Redondo Beach. In the late 1800s, most of the rancho was sold to investors. Early dry farming near and along California's coast began to wane in El Segundo when Standard Oil of California purchased hundreds of acres of its farmland in 1911. In Spanish, El Segundo means "the second." El Segundo was the site of the Standard Oil Company's second refinery on the West Coast; the first site is located in Richmond, California. The area was primarily industrial and had a Pacific Electric Rail line that ran through the town, facilitating services to and from the beach. Incorporated in 1917, the City of El Segundo is one of Santa Monica Bay's beach cities, even though it is set more inland. When Standard Oil Company established a plant in El Segundo, the city saw a boom in growth. Today, the El Segundo oil refinery has been in existence for over one hundred years, and its city is host to some of the country's largest Fortune 500 companies, including aerospace, defense and

communications industries, as well as large manufacturers. El Segundo is called "The Aerospace Capital of the World," because after World War II when many of the war-related companies transitioned into aerospace and defense industries, it created many jobs that drew people to relocate to the South Bay.

The location of Los Angeles International Airport was also part of the Rancho Sausal Redondo. The land was once used for dry farming of wheat, barley and lima beans. In the 1920s, the area was used by aviators who landed and departed on rough ground, but by 1927, local citizens wanted the city to establish an airport. In July 1927, William W.

Once comprising fields of grain and beans, this land became the airport of Los Angeles in 1930 and then a municipal airfield in 1937. Its name was changed to Los Angeles Airport in 1941 and then changed again to its final name of Los Angeles International Airport (LAX) in 1952. Today, it is one of the top-ten busiest airports in the world, ranking number six in busiest passenger traffic and in the top five for cargo traffic. It also holds the claim for "the world's busiest origin and destination airport" for 2011. *Jon B. Lovelace Collection of California Photographs.*

Mines, a real estate agent who brokered the land for James Martin—an investor who purchased a large amount of acreage—and the Los Angeles Extension Company, which Martin controlled, offered 640 acres to the City of Los Angeles for the construction of its first municipal airport. The site of the airport became known as Mines Field, and in 1952, the airport became Los Angeles International Airport, more commonly known as "LAX." Today, LAX has eight terminals and is one of the busiest airports in the country. Its unique two-tiered oval configuration allows drivers easy access into and out of the airport, or at least offers a very structured course in which to navigate in and out of the busy and often congested airport.

One of the airport's popular attractions is its eighty-five-foot-tall Los Angeles International Theme Building. An engineering modern marvel, its construction required more than nine hundred tons of steel. Construction of the building began in 1960 and took one year to

Los Angeles International Airport at night, showing its control tower and "Theme Building." Constructed in 1961 by the Robert E. McKee Construction Company, the Theme Building was considered an ultra-modern structure for its time. Resembling a flying saucer with four legs, the building contained a restaurant with a view of the runway. The building was designated as a Los Angeles Historic-Cultural Monument by the Los Angeles City Council in 1992. *Jon B. Lovelace Collection of California Photographs.*

complete. Above the building is a restaurant and cocktail lounge, where planes can be viewed taking off and landing. Atop the restaurant is an observation deck, which provides a vantage point to view the entire airport. Los Angeles's city council considered the building a cultural and historical monument, and it was designated as Historical Landmark No. 570 in 1992.

Landmarks and Points of Interest

The Lakes at El Segundo is a golf course owned by the City of El Segundo. It is known as one of the best nine-hole golf and practice courses in the country.

Chapter 7
South Bay

Manhattan Beach, Hermosa Beach, Redondo Beach and Palos Verdes Peninsula

South Bay in Los Angeles County encompasses the area in the county's southwest peninsula. It stretches along the south shores of Santa Monica Bay, including coastal areas south of Los Angeles International Airport. Sepulveda Boulevard continues from El Segundo through the community of Manhattan Beach and then enters into the community of Hermosa Beach, where it transitions into Pacific Coast Highway and continues south.

Manhattan Beach

Located south of El Segundo and north of Hermosa Beach, Manhattan Beach is a beachfront community in southwestern Los Angeles County, comprising ten miles of ocean frontage. Its land was part of the Rancho Sausal Redondo that was first sold to Sir Robert Burnett, a Scottish immigrant, in 1863. Burnett later sold the land to Canadian Daniel Freeman, who used the land primarily to grow grains. During the rancho era, the hills were primarily used to graze cattle and sheep. Two other men who are significant in the history of Manhattan Beach are George H. Peck and Stewart Merrill. Peck owned several acres of land that compose part of the north section of Manhattan Beach. Merrill, a landowner and developer, is credited with naming the town (winning a coin toss with Peck) after his hometown of Manhattan, New York. He also is credited with designing the original town site, which encompassed a large parcel of thirty-three blocks, later named Manhattan Beach Boulevard. Forty-nine years after its purchase from the rancho, the city of Manhattan was incorporated in 1912 (adding the word "Beach" to its name) and lived to celebrate its centennial in December 2012.

The Potencial Townsite Company, consisting of investors from Pasadena, envisioned Manhattan Beach as a seaside resort. A hydroelectric plant was soon constructed, which utilized ocean waves as a source of power to light an oceanside boardwalk, which later became known as "the Strand," but the problems associated with the endeavor outweighed the vision, and it was short-lived. By 1903, the Los Angeles Pacific Railroad's Del Rey and Redondo Line created a link to Manhattan Beach, allowing transportation to and from Los Angeles. It also allowed potential investors in search of endeavors to easily travel to Manhattan Beach to assess real estate and business possibilities.

Manhattan Beach Pier was completed in 1920, stretching out 928 feet; it replaced an earlier pier that was destroyed by a storm. The new 928-foot pier was constructed with cement and featured an octagonal structure at its sea end. In 1991, the pier was restored to its earlier appearance, and in 1995, it was declared a state historic landmark.

In the early years, the coastal areas in the South Bay were mostly high sand dunes, some reaching up to sixty feet, which not only narrowed the oceanfront of Manhattan Beach but also created problems for the residents living around them. Sand blew everywhere, despite measures to contain it. In the 1920s, the removal of sand and leveling of the dunes significantly reduced the sand problems that had permeated the community for years. The removed sand was used to build portions of Roosevelt Highway, later to be known as Pacific Coast Highway; as the base in the construction of Los Angeles Coliseum; and even shipped to Oahu, Hawaii, to add sand to the rocky beach of Waikiki's eroding shoreline. The removal of additional tons of sand from Manhattan's beach was used to construct the Hyperion Treatment Plant, Marina del Rey and Scattergood Power Plant. Further, combined with littoral flow that carried sand southward, it resulted in the widening of Manhattan's beach. Today, Manhattan Beach comprises two miles of white sandy shoreline.

The Strand spans the length of the beach and is popular among pedestrians, joggers and skaters. The South Bay Bicycle Trail parallels the Strand. In addition to surfing, paddle boarding and swimming, beach volleyball is a popular sport on Manhattan Beach. The Manhattan Open, a premier event on the professional beach volleyball tour established in 1960, is held at Manhattan Beach. Winners of the Manhattan Open are memorialized by a bronze plaque in the shape of a volleyball mounted on the pier.

Landmarks and Points of Interest

Manhattan Beach's pier and the Strand are its most popular attractions, including an aquarium located at the end of the pier. Around 1912, Bruce's Beach was primarily a segregated beach community comprising around two blocks on the oceanfront where African Americans in Manhattan Beach resided. Beginning in the 1920s and continuing for about a decade, racial tensions resulted in the condemnation of Bruce's Beach by the City of Manhattan Beach, forcing the African American community to leave the area. Almost eighty years later, a Manhattan Beach City Project and a Bruce family member collaborated in changing the name of the oceanfront park that once comprised Bruce's Beach back to Bruce's Beach. The project was a success, and a celebration of the name change at Bruce's Beach took place on March 31, 2007.

Hermosa Beach

Pacific Coast Highway resumes in Hermosa Beach and runs down the middle of its fifteen blocks that stretch east to west and the forty blocks that stretch north to south.

Hermosa Beach was part of the Rancho Sausal Redondo, and the area was also mostly sand dunes. Dry farming and grazing of cattle and sheep in the hills began to wane when the city began to develop. A boardwalk made of Oregon pine spanned a mile and a half along the beach in the early 1900s. After portions of the boardwalk were damaged by high tides, it was rebuilt with cement. The boardwalk

later became a popular paved path, also known as the Strand. Hermosa Beach was incorporated on January 14, 1907, and received its charter from the State of California as a sixth-class city. The Pacific Electric Red Car Line was a means of transportation that ran along the beach from Marina del Rey to the South Bay coastal beaches of El Segundo, Manhattan, Hermosa and Redondo. The city began to see more growth in the 1920s, when the Santa Fe Company built a depot for its railway and the building that became the Hermosa Biltmore

Statue at Hermosa Beach Pier dedicated to lifeguard and surfer Tim Kelly (1940–1964), whose untimely death was mourned by the surfing community in the South Bay. The City of Hermosa Beach hosts an annual Surfer's Walk of Fame induction ceremony commemorating new surfer inductees. Each surfer inductee is memoralized with his or her name engraved on a bronze plaque that is then embedded along the pier. The bronze statue of Tim Kelly marks the location of the Walk of Fame. *John Moss Photography*.

Hotel and Roosevelt Highway, later to be designated Route 1 (Pacific Coast Highway), were constructed.

Its first pier was built in 1904, constructed entirely of wood, but was destroyed in a storm and had to be replaced. A second wooden pier was constructed, but it also was damaged by storms that fatally destroyed the seaward portion. In 1945, another storm completely destroyed what was left of it. Today, the pier is one of the city's main spotlights. Surfing has a long history at Hermosa Beach, which is

In 2013, surfing great Mike Doyle was inducted into the Hermosa Beach Surfer's Walk of Fame. Also known as "Iron Man Mike," Doyle has won the World Surfing Championship, the Duke Kahanamoku title and the West Coast Surfboard Championship and was twice voted Best Surfer in *Surfer Magazine*, among many other surfing awards in the past fifty years. Memoralized by the placement of Doyle's name on an engraved bronze plaque, he joins the other acknowledged surfing notables along the pier. *John Moss Photography*.

considered to be the "original birthplace of surfing in California." Hermosa Beach was envisioned as a resort community, and the deed from the sale of the land by the Hermosa Beach Land and Water Company to the City of Hermosa Beach was written in very specific language: "That this land was to be held in perpetuity as a beach playground, free from commerce, and for the benefit of not only residents of Hermosa, but also for the sea lovers of Southern California." The city has succeeded in keeping the vision.

Unlike Santa Monica and Ocean Park that became the county's pleasure pier capital, Hermosa Beach is popular for its fishing, swimming and beach activities, including boating and surfing as early as 1933, with the formation of organized surfing in Southern California and the founding of the Hermosa Beach Surfing Club. A Surfer's Walk of Fame is located on the Hermosa Beach Pier, a tribute to South Bay's local surfing greats with their names on engraved plaques along the pier. Some of the surfing greats include Greg Noll, Hap Jacobs, Dewey Weber, Mike Purpus, Dale Velzy, Bing Copeland, Mike Stoner and Mike Doyle.

Redondo Beach

Continuing south for two miles on Pacific Coast Highway from Hermosa Beach brings you into Redondo Beach. Redondo Beach is the third South Bay city in Los Angeles County. Today, all three beach communities share a coastline and similar lifestyles and engage in the same types of beach activities, but Redondo Beach has a more colorful history.

Incorporated in 1892, Redondo Beach has a long history of being a resort community. It began with the opening of the plush Hotel Redondo in 1890. Visitors came by way of railroad and steamships to the growing popular resort and busy port. Redondo was serving Los Angeles County as its first port, and the Redondo Railway Company and the Santa Fe Railroad served as transportation to Redondo from the city and around the country. In the early 1900s, surfing was gaining popularity, and surf demonstrations were held at the hotel. The Redondo Beach Plunge was constructed in 1909 and was said to be the largest indoor saltwater pool in the world.

In 1913, a roller coaster stood north of Wharf One, the location of Redondo's current municipal pier. Redondo also constructed a dance pavilion, casino and bathhouse, which attracted many visitors. However, a combination of events led to Redondo's decline as a luxury resort and pleasure park. It began when Redondo lost to San Pedro in becoming Los Angeles's main harbor and steamships stopped calling. The railroad's termination of its line to Redondo, Prohibition and the closure of the Hotel Redondo all contributed to the continuing decline. Despite the losses, Redondo's beach and beautiful landscape still had much to offer.

Over the years, Redondo has had seven piers. There were three piers between the years 1889 and 1903 that were constructed to receive freight. In 1916, the V-shaped municipal Endless/Pleasure Pier comprised two separate parts. One section was used for railroad transport, and the other section was open to the public for strolling and fishing. Severely damaged in a 1919 storm, it was replaced in the 1920s with the Horseshoe Pier, a wooden pier that was used by lumber companies. The pier was damaged by two storms and later destroyed by fire; however, the southern Y-shaped portion of the Horseshoe Pier that survived the fire remained open. The Monstad Pier was constructed for fishing and pleasure boats but was also severely damaged by a storm. It has been renovated and is still in operation. The Monstad Pier connected to the south end of the Redondo Beach Municipal Pier. The wooden Sportfishing Pier opened in 1970 and is still in use today.

Today, Redondo Beach is popular for its harbor, marina, lagoon, piers and bicycle trail. Redondo Beach, particularly the Redondo Breakwall, is known for its surf. Record-setting fifteen- to twenty-foot wave heights were reported in 2005. King Harbor comprises four marinas and is a pleasure boat harbor. The Redondo Beach Marina attracts people year round with whale-watching trips, boat rides, sailing and sport fishing. A three-acre, seaside lagoon is popular for warm seawater swimming—the water is used to cool the power plant before it passes through the lagoon and drains into the ocean. Redondo Beach Municipal Pier features the bronze bust of California's first professional surfer and lifeguard, George Freeth, and the lower level of the pier is called the International Boardwalk. Monstadt Pier is popular for fishing halibut, bonito, mackerel, perch, sand dabs and shark. Redondo County Beach comprises two miles of sandy beach that is perfect for sunbathers and beach volleyball. It is a modern-day resort for a new generation of Californians and non-Californians who love the beach and all that a beach has to offer and a scenic Pacific Coast Highway that will take you there.

Palos Verdes Peninsula

In addition to the scenic sites along Pacific Coast Highway are the surrounding landscapes for which the highway serves as a vantage point. Before turning inland away from Redondo Beach toward the

Opening in 1954, Marineland of the Pacific was known as the "world's most spectacular circus of marine life." The landscape of the Palos Verdes Peninsula overlooking the Pacific Ocean and the beauty of Portuguese Bend were considered to be an ideal location for ecological and scientific study. Marineland's site added to the natural marine environment, displaying deep-sea fish and ocean creatures, coastal gardens and shows of killer whales, which were one of the park's main attractions. *Jon B. Lovelace Collection of California Photographs.*

city of Torrance, the Palos Verdes Peninsula cannot be missed. A detour off Route 1, taking Torrance Boulevard in Redondo Beach to Prospect Avenue South, will connect with Palos Verdes Boulevard and then connect with Palos Verdes Drive, leading around the Palos Verdes Peninsula toward San Pedro. Protruding out into the Pacific Ocean, the peninsula is home to a group of communities in its hills that includes Palos Verdes Estates, Rancho Palos Verdes, Rolling Hills and Rolling Hills Estates. From its hills, bluffs and beaches, panoramic ocean and city views are what makes this coastal area a million-dollar vantage point.

Marineland of the Pacific was once located on the tip of the Palos Verdes Peninsula Coast. An oceanarium that operated from 1954 to 1987, it sat on ninety acres and was a popular Southern California marine park. Its "Fish Tank" was considered a modern structure of its time, containing two side-by-side enormous tanks that housed thousands of fish, including barracudas, eels, sharks, stingrays and turtles. Seals and walrus performances were popular, as were Bubbles, a pilot whale, and two killer whales. In the late 1970s, Marineland became known as Hanna-Barbera's Marineland. In 1987, it was purchased by Sea World San Diego, which relocated most of Marineland's animals, fish and sea creatures to San Diego.

Landmarks and Points of Interest

Designed by Frank Lloyd Wright in the late 1940s, Wayfarers Chapel is known as "the Glass Church" and is situated on cliffs overlooking the Pacific Ocean. Next to the Point Vicente Lighthouse is a natural history museum that is an excellent vantage point for whale-watching.

Chapter 8
Torrance

Torrance is part of the 1784 Spanish land grant for Rancho San Pedro. Land grants typically encompassed vast areas of land, resulting in it being divided and sold in portions. Today, neighboring communities that were part of the Rancho San Pedro land grant include Torrance, Carson, Lomita, Gardena and Palos Verdes, formerly called Rancho de los Palos Verdes. Situated between Palos Verdes Peninsula and Redondo Beach, Torrance is also a coastal community on the Santa Monica Bay. It shares its early community development with its south bay neighbors, engaging in the dry farming of barley, alfalfa and lima beans; cattle ranching; and the import and export of goods from the nearby ports of Redondo, San Pedro and Long Beach. Later, shared efforts and contributions among the communities helped build Los Angeles County into one of the largest manufacturing centers and busiest ports in the western United States, as well as the second-most populated city/county in the country.

For over a century, Torrance was farm and cattle land. Barley, alfalfa, lima beans and oats were some of the more common grains farmed on its flat land, while cattle and horses were grazed in the foothills. When improved irrigation methods were developed, citrus, almond, olive and eucalyptus trees were grown. One of Torrance's largest agricultural ranches, over two hundred acres, was once located at the intersection of Pacific Coast Highway and Hawthorne Boulevard. By the twentieth century, Torrance and its neighboring South Bay cities helped boost Los Angeles County as a primary industry of agriculture, including fruit, dairy and poultry.

Later, Torrance became a major oil-producing region, and the city had thousands of oil wells and oil derricks scattered around it. Although the oil industry in the area significantly waned, the Torrance Exxon Mobil refinery located at the north end of the city still supplies much of Southern California's gasoline.

Incorporated in 1921, Torrance began to be populated with Portuguese, Italian, Dutch, German and Greek immigrants, as well as Mexican Americans. Most South Bay communities prospered during World War II by supporting the war efforts and later filling jobs at former wartime industries that shifted to postwar aerospace and aerospace-related industries. To accommodate the growing population, residential developments began to boom in the 1950s and 1960s. Despite the later decline of the industrial side of the community, the residential side continued to grow, attracting a large Asian population, making Torrance a multicultural community. The Mediterranean climate that Southern California enjoys, particularly its coastal communities, attracts people to live in Torrance, resulting in its becoming one of the top-ten populated cities of Los Angeles County's eighty-eight cities.

Torrance Beach

Landscaped with the picturesque hills of Palos Verdes to the south, Torrance Beach comprises one and a half miles of soft, sandy beach that is less busy than its neighboring South Bay beach communities. Also known as "RAT" Beach, "right after Torrance," because it connects with Redondo Beach, Torrance Beach joins in South Bay's long history of surfing and surfing competitions. It is the site of the annual Daily Breeze International Surf Festival, which attracts large crowds during the summer, and is popular for kite surfers and swimmers, who explore its many coves.

Landmarks and Points of Interest

Pacific Coast Highway through Torrance will take you through much of its business area, but there is so much more to this city just off the highway. The Torrance Historical Society began placing bronze plaques on Torrance landmarks, which collectively tell the story of its growth. A few of them include the Pacific Electric Railway Station, built in 1912; Southern Pacific Railroad Bridge, designed in 1913; Torrance Woman's Club, built in 1925; and its U.S. Post Office, built in 1936. Its Del Amo Fashion Center is one of the largest malls in the country, and the city is headquarters for Toyota Motor Sales, U.S.A., and American Honda Motor Company.

Chapter 9
Harbor Cities

Originally part of the Rancho San Pedro, the communities of Lomita, Wilmington and parts of San Pedro were founded when the rancho was divided and sold. Pacific Coast Highway runs through the harbor communities of Lomita, Harbor City, Wilmington and San Pedro. The landscape is industrial-residential, with oil refineries having a long history in the area since the late 1800s, when oil was discovered in Los Angeles. Wilmington and San Pedro became the main port for oil shipments and soon cargo and freight. The busy port became the city's main port, the Port of Los Angeles in San Pedro, and one of its greatest assets.

Lomita

The city of Lomita once comprised seven miles, and early visions of the area were to create a Dunkard settlement. Dunkards are members of the Church of the Brethren, which is a denomination of Christians that was established in Germany in the 1700s. When development of the land included a school, store and post office, other businesses began to sprout up, with several hundred of its acres given to the oil industry. Its claim to fame in the early years was truck farming of fruits, vegetables and eggs. Despite it being a small community, which significantly decreased from seven miles to less than two miles, it was incorporated as a city in 1964, and residents desire to keep it a small community.

Harbor City

The early 1900s marked the City of Los Angeles's plan to annex San Pedro and the harbors. San Pedro and Wilmington were independent communities and were reluctant to be annexed. In 1906, Los Angeles purchased land that connected South Los Angeles to San Pedro, naming the area Harbor Gateway and Harbor City. Los Angeles discussed constructing a port in Harbor City, but it was dismissed after both San Pedro and Wilmington agreed to annexation in 1909, leaving Harbor City as a gateway to Los Angeles's main port in San Pedro.

Wilmington

Pacific Coast Highway heads due east and meets Interstate 110/ Harbor Freeway in Los Angeles, which leads south to the Port of Los Angeles, cruise ship terminal at San Pedro and Long Beach from the Vincent Thomas Bridge.

Wilmington was first called "New San Pedro" from 1858 to 1863, until it was renamed after its founder, Phineas Banning, whose hometown was Wilmington, Delaware. Banning was a magnate in transportation services, including stagecoach and shipping. He envisioned Wilmington as becoming a major port, and his efforts led to the construction of the Los Angeles/San Pedro Railroad that spanned twenty-one miles from Wilmington's port to Los Angeles. Later, Southern Pacific Railroad in Los Angeles connected with the Los Angeles/San Pedro line and provided access to a transcontinental rail network. Wilmington became a legal port of entry in 1874, and together with its transcontinental import/ export capabilities in both rail and freight, it became America's busiest container port.

In 1942, the Los Angeles Port of Embarkation in Wilmington served the war effort as a staging area where men and supplies shuffled through the port. The first troop ship debarked from Wilmington in 1943, and it has been estimated that by 1945 more than 200,000 military personnel passed through Wilmington en route to overseas destinations. It also received the first company of WACS (Women Army Corps Service) to serve in the U.S. Army. Wilmington had three warehouses comprising 300,000 square feet each and with the capability of handling more than six thousand cars. The warehouses were located north of Pacific Coast Highway. When the California Shipbuilding Corporation, known for its building of Victory ships, began operating in Wilmington, the Los Angeles Port of Embarkation loaded more than twenty Liberty ships. Liberty ships had the capability of holding an average of twenty airplanes below decks and twelve on deck.

Wilmington proved to be an ideal harbor and port and attracted large industries that not only boosted the economy in import/export, manufacturing and employment but also put Wilmington's 9.14 square miles on the map as being one of the country's busiest ports. Oil fields and refineries also dot Wilmington's landscape. Wilmington Oil Field was established in 1932, the third-largest oil field in the country, and is still operating today, along with around eight other major refineries. In later years, the Ford Motor Company had an assembly plant on forty acres in the Cerritos Channel in Wilmington. The plant had 68 percent of its facilities in Wilmington and 32 percent in Long Beach. The plant produced cars in Wilmington until 1959, when production was moved to the city of Pico Rivera.

Landmarks and Points of Interest

During the Civil War (1861–1865), Banning and Benjamin Wilson (1811–1878), who served as a three-term elected Los Angeles County supervisor, gave the government sixty acres of land in Wilmington for the construction of Drum Barracks for the purpose of protecting the harbor. Camp Drum barracks and officers' quarters were used as the government's western regional headquarters during the Civil War. Today, it is located on Cary Avenue and is one of the two original structures still standing. It was designated by the City of Los Angeles as Cultural Monument No. 21 and California Historical Landmark No. 169, and it is listed on the National Register of Historic Places. The Banning residence, located at Banning Park, has been preserved and has also been designated as a Historical Landmark.

Wilmington's large industrial landscape showcases the economic dynamics of the large-scale import/export companies, oil producers and manufacturers that have helped build the country in general and Los Angeles County in particular. A view of the harbor's container ships at berths 134 through 147 can be seen from the Wilmington Waterfront Park.

San Pedro

Pacific Coast Highway detours away from the San Pedro Peninsula. San Pedro's highway system follows a north–south grid, mainly because of the peninsula's geography, resulting in traffic entering and leaving from the north.

Comprising 7,500 acres of land and forty-three miles of waterfront, the Los Angeles Harbor is the country's largest and busiest container port. Located in San Pedro, the San Pedro Harbor plays a major role in the growth and development of Los Angeles County. With the city's fast-growing population, by 1885, commerce in San Pedro Harbor was annually handling half a million tons of import and export cargo. San Pedro became the official Port of Los Angeles in 1907, the same year the Los Angeles Board of Harbor Commissions was created.

San Pedro Harbor, also called Timms Harbor, was once under the control of Captain Augustus W. Timms. The area of San Pedro was once known as Timms Point, the port for Pueblo of Los Angeles and the surrounding ranches. The history of the harbor becoming the main port of Los Angeles dates back to the end of the Mexican-American War (1846–1848), when the United States defeated Mexico and the harbor and surrounding areas were developed to become a working port. Phineas Banning's vision of making the harbor a main port was a success, particularly after Wilmington and San Pedro annexed with the City of Los Angeles in 1909. San Pedro, Wilmington and Terminal Island compose the Port of Los Angeles.

The fast growth of the harbor attracted many people to settle in the harbor community. Today, the community is still flavored with the tastes of Portuguese, Italian, Mexican, Irish, Greek and Croatian arrivals, to name only a few, in its many diverse restaurants. Its large multiracial community dates back to early immigrant seafarers and fishermen who once lived and worked in the harbor area.

International commerce did not reach its potential until after the end of World War I, at which time the port began to rapidly grow. Its growth surpassed San Francisco, which was the state's busiest seaport at the time. Los Angeles Harbor remained the busiest port for four decades, until the Great Depression hit. Port improvements continued during the Depression years, and later, it played a significant role in support of World War II. Shipbuilding in the port opened jobs, producing thousands of vessels in support of the war efforts.

After World War II, the Port of Los Angeles continued development of the port with new facilities, improvements in the handling of cargo and expansion of trans-Pacific trade. The cargo container that was used during the war was adopted into commercial use, which transformed the industry. The first shipment of twenty cargo containers from the port marked the beginning of the container cargo revolution at the Port of Los Angeles, which remains the leading container port in the nation. Ports O' Call, a New England–style seaside village overlooking the Port of Los Angeles in San Pedro, is the largest working port in the country. Ports O' Call is used as the departure point for harbor cruises, whale-watching cruises and sportfishing boats. Bustling with eateries offering fresh seafood, outdoor music and a million-dollar view of passing boats in the harbor, it's one of Los Angeles County's popular industrial harbor communities.

Landmarks and Points of Interest

One of San Pedro's main attractions is the museum ship SS *Lane Victory*, a Victory ship of World War II, designated as a National Historic Landmark. The Vincent Thomas Bridge, a suspension bridge that links San Pedro with Terminal Island, is the third-longest suspension bridge in California. The port's once heavily occupied military presence can be reminisced in a visit to retired battleship USS *Iowa*, the only battleship open to the public. Ports O' Call village along the waterfront is a scenic vantage point of passing boats and ships, while dining at its eateries offers many different types of seafood. The Los Angeles Maritime Museum is the largest museum of its kind in California.

A plaque marks the shipping center in the mid-1900s and was designated as Historical Landmark No. 171 in 1977. The municipal ferry building was the terminal of ferryboats that carried workers from San

Pedro to Terminal Island but was relinquished to the City of Los Angeles after the Vincent Thomas Bridge was completed in 1968. The building was designated as Historical Landmark No. 146 in 1975.

The USS *Los Angeles* naval monument located on Harbor Boulevard at Sixth Street memoralizes the men and ships of the United States Navy. It was dedicated as Historical Landmark No. 188 in 1978.

Chapter 10
Long Beach

Located in the heart of Southern California, Pacific Coast Highway runs east to southwest through the southern portion of Long Beach. It intersects with Lakewood Boulevard and Los Coyotes Diagonal, a traffic circle. Long Beach's history dates back to the sixteenth century with the arrival of Spanish explorers. In 1784, Manuel Nieto, a Spanish soldier, was granted Rancho Los Nietos by Spanish king Carlos III. Rancho Los Nietos added a large amount of land from Rancho Los Cerritos and Rancho Los Alamitos when they were parceled and sold. In 1866, Rancho Los Cerritos was sold to Flint, Bixby & Co., a northern California sheep-raising company, which was headed by two brothers, Thomas and Benjamin Flint, and Lewellyn Bixby, a cousin of the Flints. Jotham Bixby, Lewellyn Bixby's brother, was hired to manage Rancho Los Cerritos. A few years later, Jotham bought into the property and formed the Bixby Land Company. In 1880, a portion of the rancho was sold to William E. Willmore, who planned to create a farm community, but when his plans fell through, he sold the land to the Long Beach Land and Water Company.

In 1916, what remained of Rancho Los Cerritos was further subdivided into what became the neighborhoods of Bixby Knolls, California Heights, North Long Beach and part of the city of Signal Hill. Although farming had been prevalent in the area since the beginning of its founding, it began to transform and grow into a seaside resort.

When oil was discovered in 1921 on Signal Hill, Signal Hill separated from Long Beach and incorporated as a separate city. The area was rich in oil, and Long Beach Oil Field became a major oil producer, in addition to neighboring Wilmington's oil field.

Primarily industrial in the early years, Long Beach once had a large Japanese American community. Many Japanese worked on Terminal Island at the fish canneries and owned trucking businesses that transported produce from local farms.

Today, Long Beach is the second-busiest port in the country. Working together with the Port of Los Angeles, its handling of cargo, freight and containers has made Los Angeles County's harbor ports the busiest in the country.

Beaches in Long Beach

The combined beaches in Long Beach stretch over five miles and boast a beautiful shoreline. Jet skiing, kayaking, windsurfing, boat tours and sunset sails are popular water activities. Also popular along its beaches are fishing and cycling.

Landmarks and Points of Interest

Long Beach's most popular attraction is the permanently docked RMS *Queen Mary*, a 1936 ocean liner that the City of Long Beach purchased

The retired, elegant ocean liner *Queen Mary* rests in the port of Long Beach. Its first voyage was on May 27, 1936, but during World War II, it was used as a troopship, ferrying Allied soldiers until the end of the war. After the war, it was restored to passenger service until 1967, when it left Southampton on October 31, 1967, and retired. It is listed on the National Register of Historic Places and is one of Long Beach's most popular attractions. *John Moss Photography.*

in 1967. A white dome structure adjacent to the *Queen Mary* was originally constructed to house the Hughes H-4, the wooden aircraft/albatross Spruce Goose, which is now located at the Evergreen Aviation Museum in McMinnville, Oregon. The *Queen Mary* was converted into a hotel and maritime museum. Other attractions in the city include the Aquarium of the Pacific, located on Rainbow Harbor; gondolier rides through canals in its Naples neighborhood; and its front beach area, which was once the site of the Pike, a popular amusement park that operated from 1902 to 1979.

Conclusion

It has been over a century since the rancho era and a century since the first section of the coastal highway was completed in 1913, linking Newport Beach and Laguna Beach. New methods of road construction and landslide prevention are ongoing in keeping up with an expanding population and a growing need for improvements. New businesses and housing developments continue to sprout up along the coast on land where grains and beans were once grown and on hillsides where cattle once grazed. Unfortunate events through the years—such as heavy storms that demolished piers, landslides that destroyed structures, fires that destroyed homes and earthquakes that affected coastal communities and portions of the highway that runs through them—have always resulted in the rebuilding and preservation of what was destroyed or damaged.

California in general, and the coastal communities of Los Angeles County in particular, memorializes its past with many sites designated as historic landmarks and objects of historic merit. The Adamson House in Malibu memorializes the Rindge family, and the early history of Pacific Coast Highway through Malibu is part of that rich family history. Some of America's greatest singers, writers and artists resided in Topanga, and their works will remain for generations. In Pacific Palisades, Castle Rock will forever be remembered in many films in which it was used as a backdrop. Santa Monica preserves its double-jointed pier and the Looff Hippodrome. Venice Beach continues its bohemian-style community with colorful art murals and its preservation of original structures reminiscent of the Ocean Park era. Originally a desolate industrial area with oil refineries, El Segundo has grown to host some of the nation's and world's largest oil companies, aerospace industries and other Fortune 500 companies. The South Bay communities of Manhattan, Redondo and Hermosa Beaches embrace surfing histories, memorialized in a Surfer's Walk of Fame on the Hermosa Pier. The Torrance Historical Society memorializes its landmarks with bronze plaques. Much of Los Angeles County's growth was from the success of its Los Angeles Port and harbor communities. Ports O' Call in San Pedro reflects the early harbor era, and the community still comprises a large ethnic population of descendants from many immigrants who flocked to the harbor during its early construction and operation.

There are many other places and things along Los Angeles County's coast that native Angelenos will always remember and hold dear, as well as places that make tourists want to return by way of a coastal highway that can never be demolished or forgotten.

Index

A

Adamson House 23, 24, 95
Adamson, Rhoda Rindge 23
Aeroscope 48
All-American Road 11
Alvarado, Governor 44
American Honda Motor Company 83
American Riviera 12
Anza expedition 17
Aquarium of the Pacific 94
Arcadia Hotel 50
Arch Rock 24, 25
Avila, Antonio Ygnacio 65

B

Backbone Trail 21, 22, 34
Baker, Robert S. 44
Ballona Creek 65
Ballona wetlands 65
Banning Harbor 21
Banning, Phineas 86, 88
Banning residence 87
Bartolomé, José 24
Beach Club 50
Bergamot Station 55
Big Dume 20
Big Rock 21
Big Rock Beach 24
Billionaire Beach 21
Bixby, Jotham 91
Bixby Knolls 91
Bixby Land Company 91
Bixby, Lewellyn 91
Blue Streak Racer 48
Bluffs, the 65
Bob Morris's Paradise Cove Beach Café 20
Boca de Santa Monica Rancho 44
Bogart, Humphrey 28
Bonsall Canyon 22
Breakers 51
Broad Beach 14, 18, 19
Bureau of Public Roads 12
Burnett, Sir Robert 71

C

Cabrillo Highway 11
Cabrillo, Juan Rodríguez 16
California Department of Transportation (Caltrans) 8, 9, 13, 19, 29, 30, 36, 37, 39, 40, 41, 53
California Heights 91
California Incline 45
California Mission Trail 16
California Shipbuilding Corporation 87
California State Assembly 16
California State Route 1 11, 16, 36, 43, 44, 45, 57, 65, 75, 79
Camino Real, El 12, 16
Camp Drum 87
Carbon Beach 21
Carbon Canyon 22
Carrillo, Leo 16, 18
Carson 81
Casa del Mar 51
Castle Rock 41, 95
CBS studios 60
Cerritos Channel 87
Chart House restaurant 25
Chumash 16, 22, 27
city of Santa Monica 44, 53
city of Torrance 79
Civil War, the 87
Copeland, Bing 77
Corral Creek 21

D

Daily Breeze International Surf Festival 82
Dan Blocker County Beach 21
Davies, Marion 44
Deauville 50
Decker Canyon Road 21
Del Amo Fashion Center 83
de Portola, Gaspar 16
Disneyland 60
Dominguez, Juan José 65
Doyle, Mike 76, 77
Duke's 24
Dunkard settlement 85

E

Edgewater 51
El Matador 18
El Niño 38, 53, 61
El Pescador 18
El Segundo 12, 65, 66, 67, 69, 71, 74, 96
El Segundo oil refinery 66
Encinal Canyon 18, 22
Endless/Pleasure Pier 78
Escondido 21
Escondido Canyon 22
Escondido Falls 22
Evergreen Aviation Museum 94

F

Fairbanks, Douglas 45
fire 7, 18, 19, 24, 31, 40, 60, 78, 95
Flint, Bixby & Co. 91
Flint, Thomas and Benjamin 91
flood 8, 22, 23, 31, 38, 39, 53
Ford Motor Company 87
Founder's Oak 35
Franciscan Order of California 23
Freeman, Daniel 71
Freeth, George 78

G

Gabrielino-Tongva 27
Gardena 81
Geer, Will 9, 33, 34
Geoffrey's Restaurant 24
Getty Villa 42
Ginger Rogers Beach 41
Gladstone's restaurant 24
Goddard, Paulette 45
Gold Coast 44, 45
Great Depression, the 23, 51, 59, 89

H

Hanna-Barbera's Marineland 80
harbor cities 12, 85
Harbor City 85, 86
Harbor Gateway 86
Hearst, William Randolph 44
Hermosa Beach 12, 65, 71, 73, 74, 75, 76, 77, 96
Hermosa Beach Land and Water Company 76
Hermosa Biltmore Hotel 74
Highway 1 11, 43
Holiday House 24
Horseshoe Pier 78
Hotel Redondo 77
Hughes Airport 62
Hughes, Howard 62
Humaliwo 16
Hyperion Treatment Plant 72

I

Ince, Thomas 35
International Boardwalk 78
Interstate 10 57
Interstate 101 11

J

Jacobs, Hap 77
Japanese fishing 27
Jonathan Club 51
Jones, John P. 44
J. Paul Getty Museum 42

K

Keller, Don Matteo 17
Keller's Shelter 23
King Harbor 78
King Kong 23
King's Highway 12, 16
Kinney, Abbot 57

L

Lachusa Point 25
La Costa 21, 24
Lake Enchanto 22
Lake Malibu 22
Lakes at El Segundo 69
LaLanne, Jack 51
La Monica Ballroom 48
La Monte, Lou 9, 15
landslides 7, 12, 13, 28, 29, 30, 31, 38, 40, 53, 55, 95
La Piedra 18
Las Flores 21, 24
Las Tunas 21
Latigo Canyon 22
Latigo Point 21
Laudamus Hill 23
Leo Carrillo State Beach 16
Liberty ships 87
Lick Pier 60
Lincoln Boulevard 43, 57, 62, 65
Little Dume 20

Lombard, Carole 28
Lomita 81, 85
Long Beach 7, 12, 81, 86, 87, 91, 92, 93
Long Beach Land and Water Company 91
Long Wharf 41, 44
Looff, Charles 47
Looff Hippodrome 45, 47, 95
Looff Pier 45, 47, 48
Lorre, Peter 28
Los Angeles Athletic Club 27, 28
Los Angeles Extension Company 68
Los Angeles Harbor 88, 89
Los Angeles International Airport (LAX) 43, 65, 67, 68, 71
Los Angeles International Theme Building 68
Los Angeles Maritime Museum 89
Los Angeles Pacific Railroad's Del Rey and Redondo Line 72
Los Angeles Port of Embarkation 86, 87
Los Angeles Turf Club 60
Lower Topanga 27, 28
Lower Zuma Canyon 22
Lupino, Ida 28

M

Malibu 7, 8, 9, 11, 12, 13, 14, 15, 16, 17, 18, 19, 20, 21, 22, 23, 24, 25, 27, 28, 31, 95
Malibu Canyon Road 19, 22
Malibu Cove Colony 22
Malibu Creek 21, 22
Malibu Equestrian Center 25
Malibu High School 25
Malibu Lagoon 21, 24
Malibu Lagoon Museum 24
Malibu Pier 9, 21, 23
Malibu Potteries 23
Malibu Riviera 20
Malibu Trading Post 25
Malibu West 25
Manhattan Beach 12, 71, 72, 73
Manhattan Beach Pier 72
Manhattan Open 73
Marina del Rey 12, 43, 50, 57, 61, 62, 63, 65, 72, 74
Marina del Rey Beach 63
Marineland of the Pacific 79
Marquez, Francisco 44
Martin, James 68
Mayer, Louis B. 45
McCarthy-era blacklisting 33
McClure Tunnel 43
mean sea level 14
Merrill, Stewart 71
Mexican-American War 17, 88
Mexican vaqueros 17
Military Intelligence Service Memorial Highway 21
Mines Field 68
Mines, William W. 67
Minor, Lincoln 9, 23
Mission San Diego de Alcala 16
Mission San Francisco Solano 16
Monstad Pier 78
Montana Avenue 56
Mother Road 45
Mulholland Highway 18
municipal ferry building 90
Murphy, Dudley 24
Muscle Beach 51, 61

N

Neptune's Kingdom 60
Newcomb Pier 49

Newcomb, Walter 49
New San Pedro 86
Newton Canyon 22
Nicholas Canyon 21
Nieto, Manuel 91
Noll, Greg 77
North Beach Bathhouse 50
North Long Beach 91
Northridge earthquake 51
nudist club 31

O

Oberon, Merle 45
Ocean Avenue 43, 45, 56
Ocean Front Walk 61
Ocean Park 45, 50, 57, 59, 60, 61, 76, 95
Ocean Park Development Company 57
Old Topanga Fire 31

P

Pacific Electric Rail 66
Pacific Electric Railway Station 83
Pacific Electric Red Car Line 74
Pacific Ocean Park 60
Pacific Palisades 12, 13, 27, 29, 31, 34, 35, 36, 38, 40, 41, 42, 53, 95
Pacific Park 49
Palisades Beach Road 11, 44
Palisades Park 45, 53, 54, 56
Palisades Park bluffs 56
Palos Verdes 65, 81, 82
Palos Verdes Estates 79
Palos Verdes Peninsula 71, 78, 79, 81
Paradise Cove 20
Pavlik, Robert C. 8, 9
Peck, George H. 71
Pen, the 61
Pepperdine, George 24
Pepperdine University 24, 41
Pickering Pleasure Pier 60
Pickford, Mary 45
Pike 94
Playa del Rey 62, 65
Playa Vista 43, 57
pleasure park 47, 48, 49, 60, 77
Point Dume 20, 23
Point Dume State Beach 20
Point Dume State Preserve 20
Point Mugu 21, 24
Port of Los Angeles 45, 85, 86, 88, 89, 92
Portola Expedition 44
Ports O' Call 89
Potencial Townsite Company 72
Prudhomme, Leon Victor 17
Pueblo of Los Angeles 88
Puerco 21
Purpus, Mike 77

R

racing derby 59, 60
Rainbow Harbor 94
Ramirez Canyon 21, 22
Rancho de los Palos Verdes 23, 79, 81
Rancho Los Alamitos 91
Rancho Los Cerritos 91
Rancho Los Nietos 91
Rancho San Pedro 65, 81, 85
Rancho San Vicente y Santa Monica 44
Rancho Sausal Redondo 65, 67, 71, 73
Rancho Topanga Malibu Sequit 17
"RAT" Beach 82
Redondo Beach 12, 65, 71, 77, 78, 79, 81, 82
Redondo Beach Marina 78

Redondo Beach Municipal Pier 78
Redondo Beach Plunge 77
Redondo Breakwall 78
Redondo County Beach 78
Redondo Railway Company 77
Reeves, Steve "Hercules" 51
Reyes, Ysidro 44
Rindge, Frederick Hastings 12, 17
Rindge, May K. 12
RMS *Queen Mary* 93, 94
Robert H. Meyer Memorial Beach 18
Rogers, Will 40
Rolling Hills 79
Rolling Hills Estates 79
Roosevelt Highway 11, 12, 15, 36, 43, 44, 45, 72, 75
Roth, Matthew W. 9, 39
Route 3 11
Route 23 21
Route 60 11, 36, 53
Route 66 45, 46
Route 66 Preservation Foundation 45
Route 101 Alternate 11
Rustic Canyon 34, 51

S

San Fernando Valley 34, 65
San Gabriel Mountains 27
San Pedro 45, 62, 65, 77, 79, 81, 85, 86, 88, 89, 90, 96
San Pedro Harbor 88
Santa Fe Company 74
Santa Fe Railroad 77
Santa Monica 7, 11, 12, 13, 16, 22, 23, 25, 27, 28, 35, 41, 43, 44, 45, 46, 47, 49, 50, 51, 53, 54, 55, 56, 57, 60, 61, 62, 76, 95
Santa Monica Amusement Company 48, 49
Santa Monica Athletic Club 50
Santa Monica Bay 18, 20, 27, 28, 41, 66, 71, 81
Santa Monica Beach 41, 45, 50, 51
Santa Monica Canyon 44, 50, 51
Santa Monica Mountains 13, 16, 18, 20, 21, 24, 29, 31, 34
Santa Monica Mountains Conservancy 29
Santa Monica Mountains National Recreation Area 29
Santa Monica Museum of Art 56
Santa Monica National Park 21
Santa Monica Pier 43, 45, 46, 47, 50, 56
Santa Monica Yacht Harbor 48
Scattergood Power Plant 72
Schwarzenegger, Arnold 38
Scott, Reverend Charles H. 35
Sea Breeze 51
Seacomber 25
Sea Level Drive 19
Sea Lion Inn 24
Sea Shore Inn 24
Sea World San Diego 80
Secos Beach 18
Self-Realization Fellowship Lake Shrine 42
Sepulveda 65
Sepulveda, Don Francisco 44
Sequit Beach 18
Serra Retreat 23
Shearer, Norma 45
Signal Hill 91, 92
Solstice Canyon 22
South Bay 43, 67, 71, 72, 74, 75, 77, 81, 82, 96
South Bay Bicycle Trail 41, 73
Southern California Methodist Episcopal Church 36
Southern Pacific Railroad 44, 86

Southern Pacific Railroad Bridge 83
South Santa Monica 57
Sportfishing Pier 78
Spruce Goose 63, 94
SS Lane Victory (museum ship) 89
Standard Oil of California 65
Stoner, Mike 77
Strand, the 72, 74
Sullivan Canyon 51
Sunset 24, 42
Sunset Boulevard 34, 35
Sunset Pier 60
Surfer's Walk of Fame 77, 96
Surfrider Beach 21

T

Tapia, José Bartolemé 17
Tapia, Maria Merced 17
Temescal Canyon 35, 40, 41
Temple, Shirley 28
Terminal Island 88, 89, 90, 92
Theatricum Botanicum 9, 33, 34
Third Street Promenade 55
Timms, Augustus W. 88
Timms Harbor 88
Tongva tribe 27
Topanga 12, 17, 27, 34, 35, 95
Topanga Beach 27, 28
Topanga Canyon 16, 27, 28, 29, 34
Topanga Canyon Artists' Studio Tour 34
Topanga Canyon Boulevard 27, 28, 34, 41
Topanga Creek 27, 28, 31
Topanga Days 34
Topanga Earth Day 34
Topanga Ranch Market 28
Topanga State Park 29, 34
Torrance 12, 79, 81, 82, 83
Torrance Beach 82
Torrance Exxon Mobil refinery 82
Torrance Historical Society 83, 96
Torrance Woman's Club 83
Toyota Motor Sales, U.S.A. 83
Trancas 25
Trancas Beach 25
Trancas Canyon 22
Trancas Ropers and Riders 25
Treaty of Guadalupe Hidalgo 17

U

Upper Zuma 22
U.S. Coast Guard 24
USS *Los Angeles* naval monument 90

V

Vaquero Point 23
Velzy, Dale 77
Venice Beach 12, 43, 50, 51, 57, 59, 60, 61, 62, 95
Venice of America 57, 59
Venice Scenic Railway 59, 60
Ventura 12, 16, 21, 22, 43
Victoria Point 25
Victory ship 87, 89
Vincent Thomas Bridge 86, 89, 90
Virginia Reel 59, 60

W

Wavecrest 51
Wayfarers Chapel 80
Weber, Dewey 77
Westchester 43, 57
Westward Beach 20
Wharf One 77

Whip, the 48, 60
Whirlwind Dipper 48
Willmore, William E. 91
Will Rogers State Beach 28, 35, 41, 50
Will Rogers State Historic Park and Polo Club 40
Wilmington 85, 86, 87, 88, 92
Wilmington Oil Field 87
Wilmington Waterfront Park 88
Wilson, Benjamin 87
Wu, the 22

Y

Yogananda, Paramahansa 42

Z

Zuma Beach 19, 20, 25
Zuma Canyon 22
Zuma Creek 22

About the Author and Photographer

John Moss Photography.

Carina Monica Montoya and photographer John Moss are both native Californians, born and raised in Los Angeles, and childhood friends. After high school they went their separate ways, and when they reunited again after almost forty years, Carina told John that she was writing a book about Pacific Coast Highway through Los Angeles County, and John told of his decades of experience taking photographs of and surfing along the coast. The reuniting of the two old friends was providential. They collaborated on how to capture the essence of the highway in words and photographs. Together they have a combined century of personal stories and experiences to tell of the coastal road and its communities, and both have the talent and skill to add more spotlights to the famed highway, as well as the experiences of two people who have spent many years of their lives traveling on it.

Carina Monica Montoya is a retired veteran, having served in both the U.S. Coast Guard Reserve during Desert Shield/Desert Storm and the United States Navy Reserve during operations Noble Eagle, Enduring Freedom and Iraqi Freedom. She holds a master's degree in liberal studies from Excelsior College in Albany, New York, and has authored several books on California's historical communities and Los Angeles's ethnic communities.

Visit us at
www.historypress.net

This title is also available as an e-book